Muslim Faith and Values

# Muslim Faith and Values

A Guide for Christians

Robert A. Hunt

CASCADE *Books* · Eugene, Oregon

MUSLIM FAITH AND VALUES
A Guide for Christians

Cascade Books
An Imprint of Wipf and Stock Publishers
199 W. 8th Ave., Suite 3
Eugene, OR 97401

www.wipfandstock.com

PAPERBACK ISBN: 978-1-5326-6310-9
HARDCOVER ISBN: 978-1-5326-6311-6
EBOOK ISBN: 978-1-5326-6312-3

## *Cataloguing-in-Publication data:*

Names: Hunt, Robert A.

Title: Muslim fath and values : a guide for Christians / Robert A. Hunt.

Description: Eugene, OR: Cascade Books, 2019 | Includes bibliographical references.

Identifiers: ISBN 978-1-5326-6310-9 (paperback) | ISBN 978-1-5326-6311-6 (hardcover) | ISBN 978-1-5326-6312-3 (ebook)

Subjects: LCSH: Islam. | Christianity and other religions—Islam. | Islam—Relations—Christianity.

Classification: BP172 .H78 2019 (print) | BP172 2019 (ebook)

This book is the updated edition of *Muslim Faith and Values: A Study Guide for Christians* published by the GBGM Press in 2004.

Manufactured in the U.S.A. 10/11/19

# Contents

# Introduction

This book has an ambitious intent: to guide non-Muslims into an appreciation of Islam, and more importantly their Muslim neighbors. Explaining the Islamic religion is in principle fairly easy. To a greater extent than many religions, its rituals, ethical and legal principles, and basic beliefs are widely agreed. More difficult than explaining the religion called *Islam* is uncovering the faith of Muslims. Yet it is an understanding of Muslim faith that is essential to appreciating why Muslims hold fast to their religion, and the ways in which they act out their religious convictions.

In order to keep the focus of this book on the faith of Muslims, the book centers its presentations on Muslim *ideals*. These are the concrete manifestations of the character of God that Muslims speak about most often when they explain or defend their faith. It is these ideals that lead Muslims to submit to God and God's guidance, which is another meaning of the word *Islam*. It is in the course of discussing these ideals that the beliefs and practices of Islam will be presented.

In addition to what they learn in their families and communities, the ideals of Muslims are formed by and articulated in a range of Islamic literature. Most important is the Quran, followed by the *sunnah* of the prophet, the *Sirah* of the prophet, hagiographical literature, and books of law. Poetry and fiction also play an important role in shaping Muslim ideals, as does the ritual of prayer and worship. Each chapter closes with review of the key themes of the chapter and a series of readings from these various types of literature.

The intention of this book is to be useful to study groups. Short video lectures are available online on the Muslim Faith and Values YouTube channel for group and personal viewing. Discussion questions are found at the end of each chapter, following the reiteration of key themes. Further questions follow each reading. Groups may want to consider devoting two sessions to each chapter, one for discussing the body of the chapter, and another for discussing the accompanying readings. Groups are encouraged to invite Muslims to participate in the discussion. Not all Muslims will agree with authors quoted, and their viewpoints will help widen the group's understanding of Muslim faith.

Maps, a list of suggested books, a glossary, and appendixes with information on the pilgrimage to Mecca, major Muslim groups, important Muslim festivals, and the ninety-nine name of God, appear at the end of the book.

Readers should be aware that there is no standard for Romanized spelling of Arabic terms and names in English language publications. In this text the plural and singular of words commonly found in English follow the anglicized usage. Others follow the Arabic spelling and are noted in the text. For simplicity diacritical marks indicating pronunciation have not been used. Muslims terminology for some specific persons and roles differs in different languages. Here Arabic titles have been used, but readers should be aware that Muslims may use Turkish, Persian, Urdu, and Malay equivalents, depending on their own cultural background.

Dates in this book are given in two forms. Dates labeled "ah" are dates according to the Muslim calendar, which begins with the *hijrah*, or migration of the Muslim community from Mecca to Yathrib (later Medina al-Nabi). The Muslim calendar is purely lunar, and years do not correspond to contemporary Western calendar years. All dates given in the *after hijra* format are also translated into common Western calendar, and are labeled "CE" for common era if they are after the birth of Jesus and "BCE" if before.

From a Muslim point of view the Quran as such exists only in Arabic, as it was originally received by Muhammad. English versions of the Quran are regarded as interpretations rather than translations. This work uses the interpretation of the Quran prepared by Yusof Ali, unless otherwise noted. All quotations of the Quran are given in italics, and the chapter and verse are noted at the end. Readers who have, or refer to, other interpretations of the Quran should note that there are small variations in the numbering of verses (*āyāt*) between different interpretations. Many Muslim authors refer to the chapters of the Quran (*surah*) by their title rather than number. This work uses the system of numbered chapters common in most English interpretations.

Robert Hunt
Revised, Dallas 2018

# Chapter 1: Religion and Faith

On a warm humid afternoon in Kuala Lumpur, Malaysia, I sat at a table with a dozen students from the University of Malaya. We were talking about Islam, and particularly how Muslims understood Christians, and Christians understood Muslims. As we spoke, different facets of the faith of these students emerged. The name of a professor came up, and someone remarked that, "He is Muslim, but not practicing." A woman quickly replied, "Islam is a belief and a practice. If he does not does not practice what Muslims practice, then he is not a Muslim."

Her ideas about Islamic belief and practice were clearly defined in terms of the five pillars of Islam and the commonly accepted Islamic creed. The other students did not contradict her, but many wanted to add to what she said.

One young man was anxious to stress that the central tenant of Islam was the oneness of God, and for him personally Islam was a path of unity with God. Another woman reminded me that Islam was *dīn*, a way of life that encompassed not only the five pillars, but also all economic, political, family, and personal relationships. For her this was the glory of Islam, and the reason she had become a Muslim although she was born into a Buddhist family.

Another student added that Muhammad and the early leaders of Islam were an inspiration to him. He believed that only by imitating their charisma and moral leadership could modern Muslims shake off the last vestiges of colonialism. Quoting the ideas of several modern Muslim writers, another young woman stressed that Islam was a methodology for solving problems and organizing human life, not just a fixed set of rules. Finally one young man put forward that the key to Islam was the Quran. He used the prefix "hafiz" with his name, to indicate that he could chant the entire Quran from memory. For him the Quran was a miracle whose power had transformed ignorant and warlike tribes into a great civilization.

The ideas expressed by these students can be found over and again in the modern Islamic literature that most of them are reading. All of them would, at least in public, assent to the importance of the five pillars of Islam and basic Muslim beliefs. Yet it wasn't these basic beliefs and practices that most excited them most about their own faith. They were animated by a set of ideals that inspire them both to share their faith, and to work actively through various student groups to make it the dominant force in shaping their society and nation. Understanding these ideals is the key to understanding the motive power of Islam in the modern world, and why Islam has such an attraction not only for young people raised in Muslim families, but a growing number of converts as well. To introduce some of these ideals we'll look at a few of the most popular Muslim writers of this century; the ones whose books can be purchased in almost any Muslim bookstore, and which are available in scores of languages.

## 1. Mawlana Sayyid Mawdudi

Mawlana Sayyid Mawdudi was one of the founders of the influential *Jama'at-I Islami*, a Pakistan-based movement for the reform and renewal of Islam. Mawdudi's scholarship, and his commitment to making Islam the driving force behind Pakistani government, law, and society, made him a figure much admired by Muslim youth. His most popular and widely read work, *Toward Understanding Islam*, is both a primer in basic Islamic beliefs and an apologetic for the need, in the twentieth century, for a reexamination of the foundations upon which society is built.

Mawdudi articulates powerfully a central idea, and ideal, of Islam: that God's progressive and universal revelation reached its final and perfect form in Islam, and that Islam is thus the world's only truly "progressive" religion. He presents a vision of Islam as rational, forthright, and humane. It is the religion that restores God and God's law to the central place in human affairs, and thus restores both just social relations and a proper human attitude toward creation.

The focus of Mawdudi's writing is always on the principles that underlie both law and belief, and the ways in which these promote human ethics and scientific advancement. His apologetic work is frequently quoted as Muslims seek to affirm that their religion yields to no ideology in the advancement of peace, security, and human dignity. It is also controversial in asserting Islamic principles of human relationships in preference to universal understandings of human rights. But Muslims and non-Muslims are uncomfortable with his concept of a an Islamic state run on theocratic principles.

Most Muslims live in countries that are materially poor, yet have a social memory of being part of one of the world's greatest civilizations. Their powerlessness and poverty are strongly at odds with the sense of individual self-worth, responsibility, and dignity instilled by their religion. At the same time the apparent decadence, violence, and vice of the Western civilization (which Muslims see on television and read in about in their newspapers) is wedded to overwhelming power and wealth. One common explanation for this situation, adequately borne out by historical fact, is that the Muslims are victims of Western colonialism and imperialism. But why? Why should the followers of God's perfect religion be so degraded?

The answer presented by Mawdudi in his book *Come, Let Us Be Muslims,* and by many other Muslim leaders, is that Muslims have not perfectly *realized* their religion. Thus the solution to the Muslim problem is that they return to the roots of the religion, and rebuild on those sure foundations. They must more perfectly implement the great and complex system of Islam found at the height of classical Islamic civilization. Then despite their present condition, it will be Muslims alone who are destined both to shape the future of civilization and enjoy the pleasures of heaven.

One could argue that Mawdudi's vision of Islam leaves out many of the internal conflicts that so divide the Islamic world, as well as the many ways in which Muslim law and belief seem outdated and superstitious. For example, he does not talk of the problem of the Shīʿite Muslims, their persecution by the Sunni majority in Pakistan and elsewhere, or how Shīʿite beliefs fit into his model of Islam. Nor does he answer women's rights advocates apart from asserting that Islam insures a woman's "honor." But it should be remembered that Mawdudi was a reformer, not merely a defender, of the classical Islamic tradition. The inspiration he has given to generations of young Muslims came by asserting to them and for them that their tradition and their faith could build on the science and technology of twentieth-century society, while overcoming its brutality and inequality.

## 2. Sayyid Qutb

Sayyid Qutb's book *Milestones* was written while he was imprisoned in Egypt in 1965. It was widely banned, and widely read, in the Muslim world.

Its popularity was fanned by Qutb's death by hanging in 1966. It was Qutb's role in the Muslim Brotherhood of Egypt, his fierce opposition to the government, and his powerful call for the renewal of the Muslim community that led to his death at the hand of Egypt's government.

His call for renewal was based on an appeal to what he calls "The Quranic Generation," or the generation of leaders who knew the Quran and Muhammad from the beginning of the Islamic movement. These leaders knew firsthand the profound contrast between Islam as knowledge of God and the *jahilia* or spiritual and material ignorance that preceded it. Qutb believed that later generations, and particularly the current generation of political leaders, had compromised and blended the Islamic with the non-Islamic. He maintained that the twentieth-century world, including the Muslim world, was in a state of ignorance equal to that of the pre-Islamic Arabic tribes. The only solution was a radically new leadership for the Muslim community: a leadership that, like the Quranic generation, would renounce everything and start fresh with the Quran and the Prophet in rebuilding a proper Islamic society.

Qutb's appeal was revolutionary, and many credit him with having given the ideological basis for radical Islamic movements such as Hamas and Al Qaeda, as well as having provided a justification for terrorism. Yet it must be remembered that his message gained emotional strength and credibility from the fact that Muslims had for centuries idealized first four "rightly guided caliphs." All Muslim children know their heroic deeds and great works by heart. Other reformers had sought in that golden age the principles for rebuilding Islamic law and belief. Qutb focused instead on the personal transformation and commitment of those who build their entire life and life work on God's revelation to Muhammad. For Qutb's followers the golden age was neither an object of scholarly study nor a source of nostalgic comfort in the face of present-day humiliation. It was a living possibility for those who chose to dedicate themselves to the cause of Islam against a world (Muslim and non-Muslim) sunk in ignorance and degradation. Radical as he was, his radicalism was rooted in the idealism of almost every Muslim who had marveled at the victories of Muhammad and his first followers.

## 3. Ayatollah Khomeini

The image of Ayatollah Khomeini, which was burned into the consciousness of Americans and Europeans during the Iranian revolution of 1977, is almost impossible to reconcile with his popularity and influence among Muslim youth of that and later generations. In part this is because reporting on Khomeini in the West tended to focus on his anti-American and anti-Western polemics, and of course the enormous political and economic losses caused by the overthrow of the Shah of Iran. In part it was an issue of images. Muslims, and particularly Muslim religious leaders, had been caricatured in Western media for many years: until any picture of a turbaned, bearded, religious teacher was likely to summon up images of despotism, religious zealotry, and corruption. Muslim youth were not so negatively affected by either his polemic or his image. In most of the Muslim world his was the image of a respected community leader, even a saint. And his rhetoric was a declaration of independence for Islamic culture, values, and dreams.

Perhaps most importantly, he actually succeeded in setting up an Islamic republic, however problematic. For many Muslims the Ayatollah Khomeini managed to establish the beginnings of a renewed Islamic civilization. While the shortcomings of Iran have been highlighted in the West and are well recognized by Muslims, for some it has also succeeded in important ways. One of these was simply the humiliation of the United States, whose overwhelming economic and cultural influence are much resented in the Muslim world. More recently attaining nuclear power and even the possibility of nuclear weapons can be seen as restoring the power and prestige of Islam. Beyond this Khomeini managed to set up government institutions that seemed to give place to both the ideals of democracy and theocracy, neither of which existed under the rule of the Shah. And the enforcement of Islamic law in daily life seemed to create what many Muslims had always idealized, a place where Islam was truly a way of life that embraced everything from personal dress to political institutions.

The Islamic republic has not lived up to all its promises since 1979, and among Muslims and non-Muslims it is criticized for its oppression of religious minorities, lack of political freedom, and support of terrorism. It is nonetheless the only Muslim country in the world whose political, legal, and social structures are visibly based on Islamic law and tradition, and which has maintained its economic and political independence from non-Muslim nations. Khomeni's luster has dimmed with time, but the ideals of independence and fidelity to an Islamic political vision he seemed to embody still grip the Muslim world.

## 4. Fazlur Rahman and Said Nursi

Fazlur Rahman, an intellectual educated in the West, and a professor at the University of Chicago, is in many ways the antithesis of the figures mentioned above. He has not been a political revolutionary or a polemicist, and his ideas have been much appreciated by Christian and Western scholars. What makes him popular and influential in Muslim circles is his careful reevaluation of the roots of the Islamic tradition, and his call for a systematic "Islamization of knowledge."

He and others like him have tried to point out a path for rebuilding the Islamic *intellectual* tradition so that in its metaphysics, epistemology, and methodology it can replace the secular, scientific system of the West. Moreover, by working within the Western intellectual framework, and criticizing it from within, Rahman seems to point the way forward not only for Muslims, but for a larger humanity. The Islamization of knowledge as Rahman saw it wasn't just a project for Muslims, but is the restoration of human knowledge to its rightful relation with the Divine revelation.

Less known in the West, yet important in Turkish and thus European Islam, is the work of Bediuzzaman Said Nursi (1876–1960). Said Nursi received a classical Islamic education as well as learning from a number of Sufi leaders and maintaining a lifelong study of esoteric spirituality. In the late nineteenth century he was able to study modern science and philosophy and from that point onward he directed his energies to developing a theoretical basis for integrating the strengths of traditional Islamic learning, Sufi wisdom, and secular/scientific learning. He would also become active in founding schools that would put into practice the unique curriculum he envisioned.

From the advent of Kemel Ataturk's government of Turkey in 1922 Nursi was at odds with the thoroughgoing secularism of the prevailing political movement, and he often faced restrictions on his movement, or arrest. In this climate his approach to educational philosophy shifted from an emphasis on saving Islamic knowledge from its own narrowness to infusing secular knowledge with an awareness of the transcendent. What would become his most important work, the *Risale-i-Nūr*, was banned in Turkey. He was nonetheless able to establish a growing movement among educators who shared his concerns. In the last years of his life *dershanes*, or groups of students studying the *Risale-i-Nūr*, grew up around Turkey.

Eventually this movement would spread with Turkish migrant workers and become influential in much of Europe. In Turkey the Nūr movement sponsors numerous secondary and tertiary institutions, as well as thousands of study groups among students in secular universities. The closely related movement of Fetulah Gulen has, through hundreds of schools worldwide, sought to spread the idea of the compatibility of Islam with a civic consciousness in a secular society. And most recently the Swiss-Arab scholar Tariq Ramadan has taken up the task of exploring how Islam can be a European religion, and how an Islamic theory of knowledge can lead to the rebirth of Islamic social sciences.

While there is much controversy in Muslim intellectual circles about exactly how the goal of Islamicizing knowledge can be reached, and what it entails, the idea itself generates ongoing excitement among Muslims. All Muslims know of Islam's golden age, when Islamic sciences produced a vast and varied body of philosophy, mathematics, physical science, and not least juridical and political theory. Said Nursi, Fazlur Rahman, Fetulah Gulen, and Tariq Ramadan hold out the prospect of a renaissance of Islamic sciences: from the physical sciences to epistemology to sociology. And indeed a growing body of Islamic literature is available to Muslims on everything from child rearing to medicine, to linguistics, to economic theory and political science.

Numerous Islamic Universities have now been established to develop a body of Islamic knowledge comparable to that of Western universities. Conferences and seminars are held in both the West and in Muslim countries so that Muslim intellectuals can refine their ideas and influence the shape of this developing Islamic approach to knowledge. Taken together these encourage young Muslims to believe that the glory of the Islamic intellectual tradition doesn't just lie in its past, when Muslim writers of the medieval period were at the vanguard of the human quest for knowledge, but lies in a future that they will help create.

## 5. Seyyed Hossein Nasr

There has been so much focus on political developments within Islam since the Iranian revolution that developments in Muslim spirituality have often been overlooked. Yet for many Muslims the Sufi tradition provides the path to renewed faith and commitment to Islam. The Sufis saw the outward practice of Islam, and the affirmation of Islamic beliefs, as first steps toward a deeper mystical union of the soul with God. In the process of formulating their ideas, and developing techniques of meditation and communal worship, they developed a comprehensive metaphysic, a theory of esoteric interpretation of Scripture, a comprehensive understanding of human psychology, and a rich aesthetic tradition.

Seyyed Hossein Nasr, although not a leader of a particular Sufi movement, has been one of the most widely read and respected promoters of the Sufi tradition among Muslims and in the West.[1] Like Fazlur Rahman, his appeal to Western readers suggests to Muslims that their spiritual traditions have universal appeal and relevance. And his articulation of the value of these traditions within the Islamic framework underscores the completeness of Islam as a path to the Divine. Nasr's writing, like those of the growing number of Sufi masters who gather young Muslims as their disciples, complements the more strident voices for political and social reform within Islam. They remind Muslims that Islam is also deeply personal, and offers an ideal of personal transformation toward a deep inner peace and oneness with God. The success of Sufism among non-Muslims, although part of a general interest in esoteric religion in the West, has encouraged Muslims to see their spirituality as one that touches the deepest and most universal needs of the human soul.

## 6. Ingrid Mattson

Dr. Ingrid Mattson has the distinction of being the first woman to preside over the Islamic Society of North America, and is a noted scholar of Islamic law. Her popular book *The Story of the Quran* is one of the most nuanced and winsome introductions to the central experience and values of the Muslim community in print. Her journey into leadership of the Muslim community is the more remarkable because she is a convert to Islam, which she encountered while studying in France in the late 1980s. Completing a PhD in Near Eastern Languages and Civilizations in 1999 led her immediately into a professorship at Hartford Seminary, where she developed an accredited program for Muslim chaplains. In that position, and later as Chair in Islamic Studies at Huron University College, she has been tirelessly involved in encouraging interreligious dialogue, political engagement to combat Islamophobia, and combatting fundamentalist movements in Islam.

1. Nasr was University Professor of Islamic Studies at George Washington University, as well as teaching at Temple University and Tehran University.

Mattson's career is perhaps the best argument for the essential role of women in leadership in Islam, while her careful scholarly research within the Islamic tradition of legal reflection lends credibility to her feminist voice. Drawing on the work of earlier Muslim feminists, such as Fatimah Mernissi, she has been concerned to lift up the problematic issue of the role of women in Muslim society that male authors often ignore. For many modern Muslim writers the changes that Islam wrought in the misogynist structure of pre-Islamic Arabic society—insuring a woman's right to hold property, banning female infanticide, and giving women honorable roles in the family and society—are sufficient to answer the concerns of modern feminists. Yet despite the revolutionary impact of Islam on women in its early years, its classical form established a system of defined sex roles and unequal relations in which men largely controlled the lives of women.

With other feminist voices, Mattson has sought to develop a distinctly Islamic feminism drawing on women's experience that highlights the fundamentally liberating aspects of the Quranic revelation while correcting both conservatives and reformers who are content to propagate the patriarchal structures within it. Thus, for example, she interprets the traditional requirements that a woman be clothed modestly as an invitation for women to free themselves from the demeaning role of being sex objects, while asserting that no man can require this of a woman.

Her most nuanced work (some of which will be presented in subsequent chapters) deals with the contentious question of what roles a woman can or should play in an Islamic community. Some Muslim women see defined sex roles and an emphasis on the woman's role in the family as a liberating answer to the chaos of Western family structures. Others would prefer to find principles that strengthen the family without limiting the possibilities of either women or men to work and nurture their families together. Mattson clearly belongs to the latter group.

In particular Mattson takes up the role of leading prayers in the mosque, a role traditionally reserved for men in any mixed gender gathering. Rather than asserting, like Amina Wadud, that women can and should lead mixed prayers, Mattson's approach is to recast the issue in terms of the community making decisions about authority even as women assert their ability and right to participate in those decision-making processes. Her concern as a feminist is less specific roles than in placing women in the center of the processes that ultimately assign those roles.

Although Muslim feminists like Mattson have different approaches and reach different conclusions with regard to issues such as wearing the headscarf and leadership in prayers, it is the way in which they bring classical scholarship, a close reading of Islamic texts, a distinctly woman's voice, and their own capacity as leaders into discussions about the future of the Muslim community that makes Islam a viable choice for the next generation of Muslim women.

## 7. Conclusion

The Islamic religion can be defined with relative ease. It consists of five pillars that define the core requirements of both belief and practice for Muslims. And it has a basic creed that defines the doctrinal core of the Islamic worldview. These have been unchanged for over a thousand years. Yet the *faith* of Muslims, their orientation to God and their future, is far more dynamic, and is continually being shaped by their appropriation of those ideals that point the way to truly understanding and submitting to God's will. In the coming chapters we will examine these ideals in depth so as to understand something of the power that underlies the resurgence of Islam in our world, and the directions in which the Muslim community may move in the future.

## Guide for Further Study

In the first chapter you read about the idealism of many different kinds of Muslims. Review the key themes of the chapter. If members of the study group have questions about these key themes it would be good to discuss these first.

### Key Themes: Reasons modern Muslims are enthusiastic about their religion:

- They believe that Islam is a progressive religion moving humanity forward ever since the revelation of the Quran, God's final revelation.
- They believe that the example of Muhammad and the first generation of Muslims show the way for modern Muslims to overcome the willful ignorance of God found in modern society.

- They admire the idea that Muslims can live in a modern state according to Islamic law.

- They believe in the ideal of learning by integrating knowledge through revelation with knowledge through scientific observation.

- They find the possibility of achieving inner peace and an experience of oneness with God through meditation and ritual prayer.

- Some find that Islam is the force liberating women from patriarchy while showing them a fulfilling place in God's order.

## Questions for Discussion

- In your own personal experience with Muslims, or Islam, what seems to be the ideal that motivates religious life?

- Which ideals in Islam can you most easily relate to as a Christian?

- Which of the Muslim authors mentioned above seems most like Christian authors you know?

- In what ways are they similar?

- Which of them seems most different from those you know as regards their central concerns?

- What about Muslim idealism appeals to you personally?

- What disturbs or frightens you? Why?

## Additional Readings

Read the following selections from two of the authors mentioned in the first chapter, a selection from an interview with a Muslim woman, as well as the suggested readings from the Quran and Bible. Each reading is followed by discussion questions.

Mawdudi, Abul A'la. *Towards Understanding Islam*. Leicester, UK: The Islamic Foundation, 1980.

## Selections from Chapter 1.

1. This religion [Islam] enjoys the unique distinction of having no such association with any particular person or people. The word "Islam" does not belong to any particular person, people, or country. It is neither the product of any human mind nor is it confined to any particular community. It is a universal religion and its objective is to create and cultivate in man the quality and attitude of Islam . . .

   Islam, as a matter of fact, is an attributive title. Whosoever possesses this attributive, may he belong to any race, community, country, or clan, is a Muslim. According to the Quran (the Holy Book of the Muslims), among every people and in all ages there have been good and righteous people who possessed this attribute of them were and are Muslims . . .

   This automatically brings us to the question: What does Islam mean? And who is a Muslim? "Islam" is an Arabic word and connotes submission, surrender, and obedience. As a religion, Islam stands for complete submission and obedience to Allah and that is why it is called "ISLAM." (p. 1)

2. Man is so constituted that there are two aspects of his life: two distinct spheres of his activity. One is the sphere in which he finds himself totally regulated by the Divine Law. He cannot budge an inch or move a step away from it. Nor can he evade it in any way or form. In fact, like other creatures, he is completely caught in the grip of the law of nature and is bound to follow it. But there is another sphere of his activity as well. He has been endowed with reason and intellect. He has the power to think and form judgments, to choose and reject, and to adopt and spurn. He is free to adopt whatever course of life he chooses. He can embrace any faith, adopt any way of life and formulate his living according to whatever ideologies he likes. He may prepare his own code of conduct or accept one formulated by others. He has been bestowed with free will and can chalk out his own course of behavior. In this latter aspect, he, unlike the other creatures, has been given freedom of thought, choice, and action. Both these aspects distinctly co-exist in man's life.

In the first he, like all other creatures, is a born Muslim, invariably obeys the injunctions of God, and is bound to remain so. As far as the second aspect is concerned, he is free to become or not to become a Muslim. Here he has been given the freedom of choice—and it is the way a person exercises this freedom, which divides mankind into two groups: believers and non-believers. (pp. 2–3)

3. The moral life of a Muslim will always be filled with godliness, piety, righteousness and truthfulness. He will live in the world with the belief that God alone is the master of all that whatever he and other men possess has been given by God, that the powers he wields are only a trust from God, that the freedom he has been endowed with is not to be used indiscriminately, and that it is in his own interest to use it in accordance with God's Will. He will constantly keep in view that one day he will have to return to the Lord and submit an account of his entire life. The sense of accountability will always remain firmly implanted in his mind and he will never behave in a carefree and irresponsible way. (p. 25)

## Further Questions

- Mawdudi regards Islam as the universal religion because it means simply submission to God's will, which is required of all creatures. Read the Bible, John 12:32, 1 Timothy 2:3–6. How is Christianity a universal religion? How is this universal ideal different from that of Islam?

- What does Mawdudi regard as the difference between believers and non-believers in Islam? What is the difference between believers and non-believers in Christianity?

- Read the Bible, Galatians 5:13–14, 22–26 and 2 Corinthians 5:6–10. How is the Christian ideal of life different from that described by Mawdudi? How is it similar?

- Mawdudi says that humans have two aspects to their lives. Do Christians see humans in the same way?

Qutb, Sayyid. *The Religion of Islam*. Salimiah, Kuwait: International Islamic Federation of Student Organizations, 1982.

Selections from Chapter 7 (All quotations from the Quran appear as in the original text.)

1. The Arabian Peninsula was dominated by loyalty to the tribe, the sub-tribe or even to the single family, and the outside world by loyalty to country, birthplace, color and race. Humanity was unable to imagine any other kind of loyalty until Islam came and proclaimed to everyone that humanity is one, stems from the same source and is directed towards the same God; that differences of race and color, of fatherland and ancestry exist not to create division, enmity and alienation among humanity, but merely so that men might recognize and identify each other; so that the tasks of the vice-regency of God on earth might be distributed among them; and so that they might ultimately all return to God. (pp. 77–78)

> Quran 49: *O mankind, We have created you from a male and a female; And We have made you tribes and sub-tribes that you may know one another. Verily, the most honourable among you, in the sight of Allah, is he who is the most righteous among you. Surely, Allah is All-Knowing, All-Aware.*

> 4:1, 2 *In the name of Allah, the Gracious, the Merciful. O ye people! fear your Lord who created you from a single soul and of its kind created its mate, and from them twain spread many men and women; and fear Allah, in Whose name you appeal to one another, and fear him particularly respecting ties of kinship. Verily Allah watches over you.*

2. When Islam first came, human dignity was restricted to certain classes and families. As for the masses, they were but scum, deprived of any dignity or worth. Islam proclaimed with resonance the nobility of man as deriving from his very humanity, not from some incidental feature such as race, color, class, riches or position. The real rights of man are similarly derived from his humanity, which in turn derives from a single origin. . . . Thence forth people knew that man, by his very nature, was noble in the sight of God. (pp. 80, 81)

> Quran 17:70 *Indeed, We have honoured the children of Adam, and We carry them by land and sea, and provide them with good*

*things and have exalted them far above many of those whom We have created.*

*45:13 And He has subjected to you whatsoever is in the heavens and whatsoever is in the earth; all this is from Him. In that, surely, are Signs for a people who reflect.*

3. The ummah is a group of people bound together by belief, which constitutes their nationality. If there is no belief there is no ummah, for there is nothing to bind it together . . . The bond must be an idea that vivifies heart and mind, a concept that interprets being and life, that joins to God, be a breath from whose soul man became man, was distinguished from the beasts, and set aside in a God-given dignity. (p. 86)

> Quran 21:92 *Verily, this community of yours is one community and I am your Lord, so worship Me.*
>
> 58:22 *Thou wilt not find any people who believe in Allah and the Last Day and yet they love those who oppose Allah and His Messenger, even though they be their fathers, or their sons, or their brethren, or their kindred. These are they in whose hearts Allah has inscribed true faith and whom He has strengthened with inspiration from Himself. And He will admit them into Gardens through which streams flow. Therein they will abide; Allah is well-pleased with them and they are well-pleased with Him. They are Allah's party. Hearken! it is Allah's party who are the successful.*

4. However, when Islam came to associate people on the basis of belief, and made of it the principle for unity or separation, it did not make reluctance to believe a reason for hostility. It did not allow intolerance to determine its relations with those who did not embrace its belief . . . (p. 88)

> Quran 2:256 *There is no compulsion in religion. Surely the right has become distinct from error; so whosoever refuses to be led by those who transgress and believes in Allah, has surely grasped a strong handle which knows no breaking. And Allah is All-Hearing. All-Knowing.*

Further Questions

- Qutb believes that the unity of humanity derives from its common origin in God. Christians also believe that we are children of Adam. For Muslims tribal and family divisions are also God-created. Read Genesis 11:1–9, Romans 3:22b—24, and Galatians 3:26–28. How does the Christian view of the divisions and unity of humankind differ from that of Qutb?

- For Qutb it is beliefs that bind the ummah together. What is it that binds Christians together into one body?

- According to Qutb, Islamic belief cannot be forced on anyone, but persons may be forced to live within the Islamic system if they are conquered in war. How is your understanding of the ideal of freedom of religion different from, or the same as, Qutb's?

- What gives humans dignity in the view of Islam? How is this different from the source of human dignity as you understand it?

- The Quran says that Allah promises "success" to Muslims. What do Christians believe that God promises the followers of Jesus?

**Khan, Nihat Said, ed.** *Voices Within.* Lahore, Pakistan: ASR, 1992.

Excerpts from an interview with Safia: (pp. 3–23)

Q: You have a secluded society.

Safia: Yes.

Q: And you feel better for it?

Safia: Definitely!

Q: After your years of freedom when you moved easily, don't you feel claustrophobic in the veil?

Safia: I am glad you have asked this question. You see, in the "freedom" of the United States of America I felt a prisoner and in this prison I feel a sense of freedom. There whatever I was my total identity came from my husband. I was a wife and I always had to tell my husband before going out. I used to feel that in all that freedom, my freedom was being snatched from me. After coming here I feel that I have become free again. I am myself, and I am known and recognized as myself and I can do whatever I like.

Q: Does the veil give protection to women? . . .

Safia: When you talk of *purdah* you talk as if it is only for women. But *purdah*, as God ordained it, is not for women alone. God is not unjust. Where women have a dress code restriction, men are also restricted to the extent that they are to observe *purdah* of their eyes.

Q: What is the purpose of the veil?

Safia: God has created two separate domains for men and women. Women in veils feel freer. As I said, personally, I feel freer in the veil. It is important for the survival of the family. In mixed society where there is no segregation there is greater evil. A woman exploits her beauty and charm and destroys family life. The veil creates a segregated society although complete segregation is, of course, not possible.

Q: In what circumstances is it not possible?

Safia: For example, a male surgeon should be allowed to examine a female patient when there is no other choice. But it is degrading that an air-hostess should be employed on the basis of her good looks, or only women should do secretarial and advertising jobs. Both men and women must work in these professions.

Q: But coming back to male violence. How does the veil prevent that?

Safia: Islam develops an attitude. As I said, there are restrictions on males as well. Men are asked to keep their eyes lowered and not gaze at women. . . .

Q: What about the concept of the equality of women in Islam?

Safia: The concept of equality is that everyone in society has a role. Like in Pakistan there is a trend that parents want their children to be doctors or engineers. It is thought that there is more dignity in these professions. But we can't all be doctors or engineers. Society needs plumbers and cleaners too.

## Further Questions

- Safia's feelings about life in the United States would surprise many American women. Why do you think she felt that her identity came from her husband when she was in the US, but not at home in Pakistan?

- Safia asserts that Islam develops an attitude in its followers. How does she believe that this attitude is developed by the regulations regarding dress?

- What are some questions you would like to ask Safia about her faith?


Khomeini, Imam. *Love's Glance.* Found in translation at: http:// www.geocities.com/ahlulbayt14/khom-poem.html.

Some will be surprised that the Ayatollah Khomeini was a poet in the tradition of the Sufi mystics, and that his longings were not all political. Imagine if before you heard about his politics you read his poetry. What would think of his ideals?

> O my love, my world begins
> And ends at your door
> If my life be spent here
> I need nothing more
>
> In tavern, mosque, monastery
> And idol-temple floor
> I bow down in the hope that
> You would bless me and adore
>
> Not a cure could find seminary
> For my troubles nor the saint
> O get me out of mess
> With your glance ere I faint
>
> O full of ego was the mystic
> As far as I could glean
> O let me have your vision
> So my heart remains clean
>
> I have shunned my self's love
> So do I now exist
> O have your gracious look at me
> This insignificant gist

They call me man of pleasure
And they name me just a lover
O my joy-shorn heart be sure
Has never worn this cover

Life of hermit have I chosen
For that veiled darling
So that with his amorous glance
This drop be sea snarling

# Chapter 2: The Oneness of God

F rom morning to night, and deep into the night, in every Muslim land and every Muslim household the words of the *shahādah* are heard. "There is no divinity but God, Allah, and Muhammad is his Prophet."

*Tawhīd*, or the oneness of God, is the central message of Islam and an ideal shaping the whole of Muslim perceptions of the world and Muslim living. It "contains all metaphysics and also possesses the power to operate the transformation of the human soul in the direction of its primordial perfection."[1] Seyyed Hossein Nasr goes on to say, "This supreme synthesis of Islamic doctrine is, first of all, a statement about the Divine nature as being One, beyond all duality and otherness and, second, as being the Source of all reality, beauty, and goodness, of all that is positive in the universe."[2]

God's Oneness is the source of all human integrity, both personal and social; and thus not only has psychological and spiritual implications, but political implications as well. The radical reformer Seyyed Qutb, commenting on the *shahādah*, wrote, "It meant that the authority would be taken away from priests, the leaders of the tribes, the wealthy, and the rulers and revert to Allah. . . . This call to Islam was a rebellion against all modes of behavior devised by men . . . and was a declaration of war against every authority that legislates laws not permitted by Allah."[3] Whether it inspires radical Islamic reform movements, the quest for esoteric truth and spiritual ecstasy, or simply the desire to lead an integrated and meaningful life *tawhīd* is the first, and most central, of the Muslim ideals.

## 1. The Oneness of Allah

In the world of the first Muslims polytheism was the religious norm. In the heart of Mecca stood the Kaʻbah, a great stone building in the form of cube.

---

1. Nasr, ed., "God," in *Islamic Spirituality*, 312.
2. Ibid.
3. Qutb, *Milestones*, 21.

It was the center of the Arab religious world, and within it a whole range of idols representing the deities of Arab religion. One month each year all the tribes that worshipped at the Ka'bah would gather for their religious rituals as well as trade and general socializing. During that month the incessant intertribal warfare and raiding was suspended. Muhammad was probably not the only person who sensed a deep contradiction between the unity of the Arab tribes at the Ka'bah and the diversity of gods and goddesses worshipped there. Yet he seems to have seen more clearly that the worship of these multiple gods was doing little to stop the moral degradation, the descent into ignorance, going on in his time.

Muhammad received his first revelations while meditating in a cave outside Mecca. They immediately struck at the root of this contradiction with the simple message that there was only one God, Allah, and that nothing else shared the least part of Allah's divinity.

> Recite in the name of the Lord and Cherisher, who created, created humanity out of a clot of congealed blood. (Quran 96:1, 2)

> Verily, I am Allah. There is no god but I: So serve thou Me (only), and establish regular prayer for My remembrance. (Quran, 20:14)

These revelations established that God alone was creator of humanity and its Lord, and goes on to demand that the self-sufficient people of Muhammad's day return to reliance on God, praise him only, follow his path, and thus escape judgment.[4]

The Quran, which contains the revelations received by Muhammad, regards this as no new message. It is identical with the religion established by Abraham and Moses. Those verses that attack idol worship and polytheism most clearly come when the Quran recounts their stories. It is with Abraham's words that the Quran speaks:

> Serve Allah and fear Him: that will be best for you—If ye understand! For ye do worship idols besides Allah, and ye invent falsehood. The things that ye worship besides Allah have no power to give you sustenance: then seek ye sustenance from Allah, serve Him, and be grateful to Him: to Him will be your return. (Quran 29:16–17)

---

4. Muslims almost uniformly use masculine pronouns for God. It is not that they ascribe a sex or gender to God, but because in the Arabic of the Quran God is always referred to using masculine forms. Thus they are true to the language of the Quran without accepting any implication of comparing God to humans.

Allah, as Muhammad experienced him in the revelations of the Quran, was an utterly transcendent Deity, far above and distinct from everything of the world. The oft-heard declaration of Islam, *"Allah u akbar,"* "God is greater," begins every call to prayer and punctuates every speech or sermon. It proclaims this transcendence in relation to the world and its powers as well as every human ideology or idea.

*Shirk,* the sin of making anything equal to God, is the most serious in Islam. The "unbeliever" or *kāfir* is not an atheist, but a polytheist or idolater. So Muhammad was commanded: *Say: He is Allah, the One; Allah, the Eternal, Absolute; He begetteth not, nor is He begotten; And there is none like unto Him.( Quran 112)*[5]

Although utterly transcendent, Allah was not a distant ideal without connection to human life. God's knowledge of a person's heart is intimate. *"It was We who created man, and We know what suggestions his soul makes to him: for We are nearer to him than (his) jugular vein." (Quran 50:16)*

God's law is immanent in all of creation, and is reflected in every aspect of the natural world, which by nature submits to God's will. *"To Allah belong the East and the West: whithersoever ye turn, there is Allah's face. For Allah is All-Embracing, All-Knowing." (Quran 2:116)*

By encouraging Muslims to see in nature the signs of God's presence, creativity, and omnipotence these and other verses helped spur the development of Islamic science and were a powerful force in shaping the esoteric mysticism of the Sufis. For Muslims the poet, overwhelmed by the majesty of nature, the scientist intrigued by its complex workings, and the mystic in rapt inner contemplation of the unity of all existence all three worship the One God, Allah. This also is a powerful witness to the meaning *tawhīd* and the extension of God's oneness into the human realm.

5. This last verse, translated into English, seems like a direct attack on the Christian belief expressed in the Nicene Creed "I believe in one Lord Jesus Christ, the only begotten Son of God." And some modern Muslims quote this verse in polemical attacks on Christian doctrine. The Quran itself attacks the idea that God would have physically originated a child. Yet it must be remembered that the Nicene Fathers tried to overcome exactly this kind of misunderstanding and misinterpretation of Christian belief by using abstract philosophical language. Christians and Muslims need to remember that there was a vast difference in worldview and understanding between the Greek and Latin Church fathers who composed the creeds and that of Arabic-speaking Muhammad. Both wished to insist on the integrity and unity of God. Moreover, in the Quran both Christians and Jews are regarded as part of the monotheistic family from which Islam comes, and Christians in particular are called "the nearest among them in love to the Believers." Facile translations of widely different texts, which are historically and culturally far removed from one another, are a poor basis for comparing beliefs.

## 2. Unity and Theology

The Quran does not stick to philosophical niceties in its powerful, poetic representation of the depth of God's immanence and the height of God's utter transcendence and sovereignty. Frequently it uses anthropomorphic language to describe God and God's activities. The beauty of the Quran and its effect upon the first generation of believers overpowered considerations of theological consistency and precision of language, and for many Muslims this remains the case up to today. The Hanbali school of Muslim law and theology (one of four recognized by Sunni Muslims) simply refuses to play off revelation against theological rationalism, letting the apparent inconsistencies between claims of transcendence and anthropomorphic representations of God point to a mystery beyond the human capacity to understand. This is for them the essence of revelation.

The opposite extreme was found among the Muslim theologians who first encountered Greek philosophy. The Greeks spoke of a God knowable to all humans through the universal language of reason. Like the Quran their philosophy affirmed the unity, transcendence, and immanence of God. But it sought to define these ideas with precise language and logically related concepts. For the *faylahsufs,* or Muslim philosophers, the Quran needed to be interpreted in conformity with the rational and ethical norms that every human could affirm by reason alone. This, they believed, was consistent with the claim that Islam was God's universal religion.

However, the conclusions they drew seemed to contradict not only the literal meaning of the Quran, but also some cherished beliefs of Muslims. One philosophical school, the Mu'tazilites, believed that a rational faith in God's justice and human freedom overturned the common Muslim belief that God predetermined all events, including death and judgment. Others followed the lead of philosophers such as Plato and saw God's relationship to the world in terms of emanations from the divine essence through several levels of existence. This remains a popular concept among Muslim mystics. Yet for early theologians such as al-Baqillani (940–1030 CE) this seemed to suggest that some things could exist apart from Allah. He maintained that everything in existence, in its most particular form, related moment-by-moment directly with God through God's will.

---

*O God,*
*You know that the only thing*
*I want in this life*

*is to be obedient to your command.*
*Even the living sight of my eyes*
*is service at your court.*

*The poet Rabi ʿa al-Adawiyya, (713–801 CE) one of Islam's great*
*woman mystics*

---

Al-Baqillani belonged to what would become a dominant approach to Islamic theology: that of al-Ashʿari (874–836 CE). It attempted to develop a rational and systematic theology while affirming the Quranic assertions of God's absolute omnipotence and omniscience. In doing so it established the limits of what human reason and power could expect to accomplish by reflecting on God's revelation.

For theologians of the Ashʿari school, revelation was critical to human morality. They believed that the categories of good and evil correspond to God's will rather than human notions of good and bad. Thus they provided an answer to the haunting question of how God can allow what appears to be evil: God is beyond human moral perceptions and distinctions. With regard to human freedom al-Ashʿari maintained that God creates the deeds humans do, yet it is humans who freely appropriate them and stand liable for them at the judgment day. As strange as it may sound to modern ears, this idea of taking personal responsibility for what God has preordained has inspired many Muslims to a deep spirituality of surrender to God's will.

---

*What the Lord expects of His vassal is that he be the form in which*
*His action and His influx are manifested. The vassal accomplishes*
*His will (acknowledges his Lord) by the mere fact of his receptivity*
*as a form manifesting His suzerainty, and he is acknowledged by*
*Him thanks to the mere fact that he manifests this suzerainty. He*
*has no action outside of his receptivity which accomplishes the*
*intention of his Lord.*

*Ibn al-Arabi (1076–1148 CE)* [6]

---

Nor is this spirituality a remnant of Islam's past. The teaching of *qadāʾ/qadar,* or the acceptance of God's predestination, was central to the conversion of many people from a nominal to more serious commitment to Islam. This kind of acceptance of predestination was also part of the great evangelical

6. Corbin, *Alone with the Alone,* 311–12.

Christian revivals in New England and England in the eighteenth century, and was central to the spirituality of Calvinist Christianity. *Fate* is a much maligned word in the West; *destiny*, no different, is somehow more desirable. Surrender, which both fate and destiny require, has always been part of the monotheistic spirituality.

## 3. The One Faith

For Muslims the Oneness of God implies the continuity of God's revelation in history. The first prophet of Islam is none other than Adam, the first human. While traditionally seen as a man, the feminist Muslim leader Amina Wadud (b. 1952) points out that "Adam" stands for undifferentiated humanity, of which men and women are complementary parts. Thus, the whole of humanity is charged with the truth of God's Oneness. "Prophet" is not gender specific.[7] According to the Quran, other prophets followed. Most of those named are familiar to Jews and Christians, and include Abraham, Moses, and Jesus. Equally important are the unnamed prophets, which in Islamic tradition number in the thousands or tens of thousands. Every people in every age are united in having been sent witnesses to *tawhīd*. There is, for humankind, only one true revelation corresponding to the One God.

This does not suggest that all religions can be seen as manifestations of Islam. The Quran is adamant in its condemnation of polytheism and any form of religion running contrary to God's unity. Some early Muslim leaders, when they conquered non-Muslim territories, required those who were regarded as polytheists to convert to Islam. Yet the concept of Islam as the universal religion of humankind, revealed in a diversity of times and cultures, was also a means by which diverse religious faiths could be accommodated within Muslim rule. Zoroastrianism, initially regarded as polytheistic, was finally accepted as a legitimate expression of God's revelation for a certain people.

> And among His Signs is the creation of the heavens and the earth,
> and the variations in your languages and your colors: verily in that
> are Signs for those who know. (Quran 30:22)

Eventually even Hinduism, with its myriad of idols and pantheon of gods, could be rationalized as monotheistic by focusing on the underlying

---

7. Wadud-Muhsin, *Quran and Woman*, 15.

understanding of Brahman as the undifferentiated reality beneath and beyond all human and divine manifestations. Modern conflicts between Muslims and Hindus mask a long history of fruitful encounter that enriched Muslim mysticism and eventually gave birth to a whole new monotheistic religion: Sikhism. In modern times Muslims have quoted the Buddha and Confucius as prophets of Allah for a certain people in a certain time. The Quran itself says that the cultural and racial diversity of the human community is a sign of God.

## 4. The One Community

> *Verily, this Ummah of yours is a single Ummah, and I am your Lord and Cherisher: therefore serve Me (and no other). (Quran 21:92)*

While diversity in human culture is a sign of God's bounty and an encouragement for humans to strive to imitate and exceed their betters, the revelation of the Quran to Muhammad is seen by Muslims to usher in a new age. God's ultimate intention is that humanity be united under the final and comprehensive relation of the Quran, and in the single religion of Islam. Other monotheistic religions could be accommodated as Islam spread, but finally the religion of Muhammad and the Quran would visibly unite the diversity of humankind. Diversity is also a product of human hard-heartedness.

> "Mankind was one single nation, and Allah sent Messengers with glad tidings and warnings; and with them He sent the Book in truth, to judge between people in matters wherein they differed; but the People of the Book, after the clear Signs came to them, did not differ among themselves, except through selfish contumacy. Allah by His Grace Guided the believers to the Truth, concerning that wherein they differed. For Allah guided whom He will to a path that is straight." (Quran 2:213)

> That guidance comes with Muhammad. "It is He Who has sent His Messenger with Guidance and the Religion of Truth, to proclaim it over all religion: and enough is Allah for a Witness." (Quran 48: 28)

For Muslims the unity of *ummah*, the community of believers, is a central witness to the unity of God. And in the Quran Allah condemns those who divide the *ummah* and question the Prophet and Quran.

CHAPTER 2: THE ONENESS OF GOD

From the beginning this insistence on the unity of the *ummah* as an ideal linked to the ideal of *tawhīd* has inspired both Muslim politics and theology. When upon the death of Muhammad certain Arab tribes tried to withdraw from the *ummah* they were forcibly subdued and brought back into the fold of Islam by Abu Bakr (573–634 CE).

In 661, the Muslim community was decisively divided between the partisans of Muhammad's nephew Ali (601–661 CE) and those of the Prophet's companion Muawiyya (602–680 CE). Yet in a way each preserved the ideal of unity by regarding the other as *kāfir*, as having left Islam rather than dividing it. The Shiites, or partisans of Ali, would lose the last of their political leaders and develop an eschatological hope in a coming *Imam* who would restore the unity of the Muslim community. The Sunni Muslims, descendants of the partisans of Muawiyya, would maintain that the *ummah* was always united under a single Caliph who was a direct political descendant of Muhammad.

Despite the real fractures of the Islamic political world the fiction of a single head of all Muslims was maintained by successive Muslim dynasties right up to the twentieth century. It was ended only when secular Turkey, the successor to the Ottoman Empire, abolished the Caliphate in 1924. Even then Muslims from around the world gathered on several occasions in an attempt to revive this unifying institution. Today, while the vast majority of Sunni do not accept that any leader can presume the title "Caliph," many Muslim political theorists regard the institution itself as necessary when an authentic Muslim state is established.[8]

In the twentieth century here has also been an official rapprochement between Shiites and Sunni Muslims, although sectarian violence remains endemic in some Muslim lands. They have been able to accommodate one another's traditions by regarding the particular tradition of the Shī'ite minority as a fifth "school" of law and theology within a united Islamic tradition. As both Shiites and Sunnis look forward to the restoration of Islam's political unity, they may also see Imam and Caliph as a single hope.[9]

8. Sardar, *Islamic Futures,* 333.

9. One group of Shiite Muslims, the Ismailis, believe their leader the Agha Khan (IV) is the true successor of Muhammad and Ali. However, he makes no claim to political power and acts as spiritual leader only of his people.

## 5. The One Path

Religion, as used in the verses of the Quran above, is not for Muslims merely an inner attitude of faith or a set of firmly held beliefs. Frequently Islam is referred to as *dīn*, meaning religion, but often interpreted in English as "a way of life." It is the way of life pioneered by Muhammad and captured immediately and vibrantly in the *sunnah* (tradition) of the Prophets' words and actions. It is enjoined upon all who submit to God. Fully articulated this way, or *Sharia*, (whose root word is *path*, or *road*) is a complex and variegated law governing every aspect of human behavior (see chapter 6 below). At its center, however, are the five pillars of Islam, each of which both unifies and is a sign of unity.

The first of these is the *shahādah* mentioned above, which declares the unity of God and the primacy and finality of Muhammad and his religion. The others are found in various places in the Quran, and their centrality is confirmed by a *hadith* (tradition relating the words of Muhammad, as opposed to the Quran) stating:

> *The Messenger of Allah (peace be upon him) said: "Islam is to testify that there is no god but Allah and Muhammad is the Messenger of Allah, to perform the prayers, to pay the zakāt, to fast in Ramadan, and to make the pilgrimage to the House if you are able to do so."* [10]

### Prayer

Imagine for a moment that you sleeping soundly in a suburb of a city in central Java. As the sun rises, the sound of birds calling and roosters crowing is overtaken and overwhelmed by the rhythmic call of drums from a dozen small mosques in the neighborhood. More distant is the amplified call from a large mosque: "*Allahu Akhbar!*" The melodic chant with which the *muezzin* sings his call is familiar, for it can be heard from Chicago to Jeddah to Lahor to Bangkok to Yogyakarta: wherever Muslims live and gather for prayer. Men and women make their way to the nearest mosque, or simply lay out a rug on the floor of their house. As the call of the minaret dies two million voices in that city begin to rise in prayer: the same prayer in the same language. They prostrate themselves, then rise and then fall again in a rhythm so ancient and universal that it seems timeless—although it was established a mere 1,400

10. Muslim, *Sahih Muslim*, Vol. 1, Book 2, Number 7.

year ago. In ten minutes, fifteen at the most, they are finished and begin to go about their daily work. But a few dozen miles to the east another group of Muslims is rising and repeating the ritual, and then another. When the last Javanese Muslim is finishing work in the evening American Muslims in Chicago or Los Angles will be rising to continue their rite. In twenty-four hours the call of the minaret, the acclamation of God, and prostration of Muslims in prayer will have swept over the earth five times and joined over a billion people in worship of Allah.

This unity did not come at once, but by the time Muhammad passed away (632 CE) the Quran and the Prophet's own practice had revealed both how and when Muslims should pray, which direction they should face (toward Mecca), and exactly what they should say. They would be called to prayer with the declaration that "God is Greater" and would begin their prayers by saying,

> *In the name of Allah, Most Gracious, Most Merciful. Praise be to Allah, the Cherisher and Sustainer of the worlds; Most Gracious, Most Merciful; Master of the Day of Judgment. Thee do we worship, and Thine aid we seek. Show us the straight way, the way of those on whom Thou hast bestowed Thy Grace, those whose (portion) is not wrath, and who go not astray. (Quran 1:1–7 )*

The prayer is said in Arabic, even by those who do not understand the language. (All Muslims understand its meaning.) It comes directly from the Quran, and thus it has none of the divisive force of an expression of mere human feelings, and all of the unifying force of God's unchanging Word. Following this opening prayer each Muslim performs a repeated series of bows and prostrations, during each of which a short set of verses from the Quran are recited. Between each of these sets the unity and majesty of God are declared, and God is praised. For those who worship in the mosque, or on a public square, the unison bowing and prostration link them, like the sound of the *Fahtiah* (opening *surah* of the Quran) with every other Muslim in the world, or who has ever lived. The ritual allows time for personal and intercessory prayers, and requires an inner intention to match the outward act. Yet above all it is an act of obedient remembrance (*dhikr*) of unity, the Unity of God and of the one *ummah* of the one God united together and with God in obedience to God's command.

## Almsgiving

*Seest thou one who denies the Judgment (to come)? Then such is the (one) who repulses the orphan, And encourages not the feeding of the indigent. So woe to the worshippers who are neglectful of their prayers, those who (want but) to be seen, but refuse (to supply) (even) neighborly needs. (Quran 107)*

Islam requires that each believer give a fixed sum, based on their income, to the support of the poor, those with burdensome debts, travelers in need, and to redeem slaves. Throughout the Quran the giving of alms is associated with both the prophets of the one God, Allah from Abraham to Moses to Jesus, and with authentic worship. Numerous verses equate it with submission to Allah and reinforce its role as a pillar of faith. Almsgiving is said to purify wealth and keep believers from becoming enamored of their material possessions and self-reliant rather than reliant on God.

At a deeper level the giving of alms both unifies the *ummah* and is a sign of that unity. Muhammad was born into a culture whose people were totally dependent on their clan for survival, and the clan supported every member in need. The first Muslims were often persecuted within their families and clans, and depended on one another. God's command that a fixed portion of income would be distributed to the needy in the community perpetuated the value of interdependence found in Arab culture while breaking down the petty clan and tribal loyalties that so bedeviled Arab unity. Institutionalizing almsgiving also underscored the egalitarian ideal of Islam, allowing the poor the dignity of drawing from a common fund rather than becoming clients of wealthy individuals. And as the *ummah* was to ultimately be identical with all humanity, almsgiving was a sign of a common human obedience to, and dependence on, God alone.

## Fasting

Muslims are required to fast from sunrise to sunset during the month of Ramadan. During that time they abstain from both food and water, and according to some teachers from sex and smoking as well. Numerous exceptions—for those traveling, for small children, for the sick, and for pregnant women—underscore the fact that this is no ascetic discipline. Nowhere in Islam is the body per se a danger to human spiritual health. It is not the appetite, but the will, which needs training.

The primary purpose of fasting is therefore to simply submit to God's command. Some Muslim schools of law forbid fasting once the day is ended, lest any Muslim believe himself or herself more pious than others. Muslims are also taught that their own hunger during the fast makes them more aware of the poor among them, and they are encouraged to share food with those whom they have shared hunger.

Watching daily life in a Muslim society there can be little doubt of the community-building role of the fasting month. Young children look forward to being old enough to participate in the fast, and thus fully enjoy the festival atmosphere when the fast is broken each evening. The exact times at which the fast begins and ends (determined in modern times by astronomical calculations) are posted publicly. More than any other time of year Muslims gather in the evening, usually for a nightly feast which breaks the fast. Traditional foods for breaking the fast like dates and mutton, which must be imported in Muslim Southeast Asia, link Muslims worldwide in a common culinary experience. At the same time it is a month in which every Muslim culture will show off its particular delicacies, and every Muslim cook his or her specialties.

In the middle of Ramadan Muslims celebrate the "Night of Power" on which the Quran first descended upon Muhammad. Leading up to that night large portions of the Quran are read in every mosque. On the Night of Power itself those who are able to do so recite the entire Quran by memory, while others listen. The unity of the fast thus refocuses Muslims on the unity of God's revelation and their own participation in the prophetic experience.

The need, and indeed the demand, for unity through fasting is underscored by the coercive approach of Muslim governments toward fasting. In much of the Muslim world it is against the law for men or women to publicly ignore the fast without reason. Religious teachers who contradict the official day on which Ramadan begins and ends, or the daily times each day, face criminal charges and imprisonment. This, and the elaborate observations and calculations necessary to establish fasting times down to the second can appear either picayune and legalistic or earnest and faithful, depending on one's preconceptions about what constitutes religious faith. For Muslims an individual sense of submission can never displace the sheer demand of God that unity be reflected in public obedience as well. The human being, personally and socially, is united.

Pilgrimage

At a mosque in Atlanta, Georgia a preacher looks out at his congregation. Most, like himself, are African Americans. Yet there are also many Pakistanis, Africans, Indonesians, and a smattering of Europeans. Their various cultural backgrounds are manifest as they respond to the words of the sermon. The Asians and Europeans are somewhat reticent, while the Indians and Africans call out *"Allahu Akhbar"* lustily. Many of the African Americans shout "Amen." The preacher is speaking about the Hajj, an event central to Muslim spirituality and at the axis of African American Islam.

In 1964 Malcolm X (1925–1965), fiery orator for the Nation of Islam, made his pilgrimage to Mecca. There he discovered the ways in which Nation of Islam doctrine varied from that of orthodox Sunni Islam. Most importantly he found a vast gathering of people of all races and cultures, joined in a single ritual without regard to social status and without prejudice. It was a powerful witness to what unity meant in Islam. He returned to America with a new name, El Hajj Malik el-Shabazz, and a new vision of human unity that broke with the Nation of Islam.

The Atlanta mosque is in many ways the spiritual child of the conversion of el-Shabazz. The preacher, himself a recently returned pilgrim, described the great rite in which millions of Muslims from every nation rose and fell together in prayer. He spoke of a flower blossoming with every color and fragrance of the garden of the world. He described the way in which the faithful circled the *Ka'bah* as a vast wheel in which each Muslim spiraled toward complete unity with God and then moved outward into a world to be united in Islam. Born into a world where prejudice and discrimination were daily experiences, and racial hatred a common ideology, the preacher had found in Islam, and in the Hajj, a compelling ideal and vision of humanity under the one God.

The social dimensions and possibilities of that unity are worked out in places like Atlanta when Muslims gather their resources to build private schools, community centers, and mosques. In this they fulfill Muhammad's intention for the Hajj, which was to unify both Arab Muslims and all monotheists. According to the Quran, Abraham is the founder of the pilgrimage to the *Ka'bah*, making the Hajj the first of all religious rituals, and the great witness to the Oneness of God.

The model for the modern Hajj, with its six days of ritual activities, is the two pilgrimages Muhammad made after establishing Islam. On the first the non-Muslim Arabs who still controlled Mecca were obliged to allow those loyal to the Prophet to make their religious rituals in peace. On the second, shortly before Muhammad's death, Mecca was Muslim, and all of Arabia was united behind him. From that time forward Muslims have made the Hajj, participating in rituals reinforcing their fundamental orientation to God and the world, and experiencing the equalitarian and unifying ideals of Islam. (See Appendix A.)

Through the centuries the pilgrimage has served not only to unify Muslims, but also to spread movements of political and spiritual reform throughout the Muslim world. In the centuries before mass transit and rapid communications the outlying parts of the Muslim world in Southeast Asia, pilgrims drew the subcontinent, Central Asia, and Africa into the movements sweeping Islam. They brought news and new ideas home after lengthy stays in the Holy Land.

Over the centuries many of the Sufi movements spread outward as pilgrims became disciples of *pirs* (Sufi teachers) living in the region of Mecca. For many of them a pilgrimage to Mecca served the dual purpose of fulfilling an Islamic obligation and providing a chance to pray at the tombs of great saints and imbibe their blessings. After the *Wahhabi* movement "cleansed" Mecca of such practices, its ideal of reform also spread through a network of pilgrims, sparking nineteenth-century political and social revolutions from North Africa to Java. In the last two decades Iranian pilgrims have sought to use the Hajj to spread the ideals of the Iranian revolution across the world. This politicizing of a great religious ritual is repugnant to those Muslims who seek a deeply personal sense of communion with the Divine. Yet it is not alien to either the origins or history of the Hajj. Unity in Islam has always been sought at every level of human existence.

## The Creed

The Pillars of Islam were a fundamental expression of Muslim unity by the end of the Muhammad's life. In succeeding centuries, in the face of powerfully divisive theological movements, creeds were adopted giving Muslims a unified set of doctrines. They are based on a *hadith* that tells how the Prophet answered about true faith:

> *"The Prophet (may the blessings and peace of Allah be upon him) said: 'It is to believe in Allah, His angels, His books, His messengers and the Last Day, and to believe in divine destiny, both the good and evil thereof.'"*

33

*The basic Muslim beliefs are:*

*The oneness of God*

*The Angels*

*The Books of God*

*The Prophets of God*

*The Final Judgment*

*Predestination*

Unlike Christian creeds, the creeds of Islam play no role in public worship, and both the exact number of their provisions and their interpretation remain open.[11] Yet in an idealized system they complete the knowledge system of Islam. A Muslim living by the five pillars is perfected in religion, by the creed is perfected in faith, and by the law is perfected in social relations. When a modern Muslim says that Islam is a practice and a belief, he or she is echoing this theme, and an insistence in some Muslim movements for not only orthodox practice, but doctrine as well. The basic beliefs given below are not found in all creeds, but are commonly listed.

## The Oneness of God

As noted above, the oneness of God is central to Islam. In the classical creeds this is further defined to say that God is:

- Absolute—all that is other is nothing, God bestows existence upon non-existence and creates the distinction between real and unreal.

- Infinite—and thus includes all that is and is possible within God's self.

- Perfect—possessing every possible perfection, and thus the source of all quality.

---

11. Al-Ashari in the early tenth century and ash-Shafi'i in the early ninth produced influential creeds. The six fundamental items in these creeds and others are discussed in this section.

- Transcendent in Oneness—God is greater than whatever is affirmed or asserted about him.

- Immanent in Oneness—"Wherever you turn, there is the face of God." (Quran 2.115)

Some creeds also list the ninety-nine names of God as part of the basic beliefs of Muslims. (See Appendix D.)

## Angels

Angels appear frequently in the Quran, and belief in them is thus fundamental to a Muslim worldview. They are the messengers of the unseen world, as well as having many other functions. Muslims believe in a number of specific angels, including Gabriel, Michael, Izra'il (the angel of death), the Cherubim, two guardian angels for each person, the angels who question the dead in the grave, and fallen angels who along with Iblis (Satan) are responsible for much temptation and evil. This extensive angelology helps explain how God relates with humans without implying that God's unity or singularity is violated.

Angels are only one part of the world of invisible creatures. Another is the *jinn,* from which the English word *genie* derives. The *jinn* can be good, bad, and indifferent to human affairs. Despite the fact that the Quran specifically discourages human intercourse with spiritual beings many Muslims are fascinated, and terrified, by the possibility of possession and oppression by spirits. Throughout the Muslim world *jinn* are called upon for the favors and power they can bestow, and feared for the harm they can do.

## The Books of God, or Kitab

The Quran is explicit in saying that there exist other books of God's revelation. It explicitly names the *Zabūr* or Psalms of David, the *Taurat* or Law of Moses, and *Injil* or the words of Jesus. It suggests the possibility of many others as well, each the product of one of God's prophets. Muslims believe that the Quran has now surpassed all the others and contains the summation of their wisdom in pure form.

## The Prophets of God

Traditionally the number of God's prophets throughout history is 200,000. They are the founders of all the monotheistic religions. Hence Muslims may be critical of other religions, which have become perverted by human weakness, but never their founders, lest they be disrespectful to a prophet of God. A number of these prophets are named specifically in the Quran, and a few are given special titles: Adam: *Safiyu'llah*, chosen of God; Noah, *Nabiyu'llah*, the prophet of God; Abraham, *Khalilu'llah*, the friend of God; Moses, *Kalimu'llah*, the one to whom God speaks; Jesus, *Ruhu'llah*, the spirit of God. Muslim interpreters of the Quran regard this title as a reference to the angel Gabriel, who was always near Jesus. Thus the title does not mean for Muslims what it might mean for Christians.

Finally there is Muhammad, *Rasulu'llah*, the messenger of God. Each of these prophets is a leader of his dispensation, and in popular belief each will intercede for his followers on the Judgment Day. In the Quran only Jesus among the prophets is sinless. There are traditions suggesting, however, that God removed any sin Muhammad might have and in popular belief he is sinless as well.

## The Final Judgment

### 1. Death and the Grave

Islam is a way of life. But this way of life was always a way *to* eternal victory, reward, and success in the form of promised *al-Jannah*, paradise, or literally "Garden." This way leads through death and the grave, and God's judgment, before reaching its end with either eternal bliss or eternal suffering. By the time Islamic theologians developed the first creeds Islam had a highly developed doctrine of punishment in the grave (*'adhāb al-kabr*). The tradition states that two angels, *Munkar* and *Nakir*, will examine each person after death regarding Muhammad (or in a more elaborate form, God, Muhammad, religion, and direction of prayer). The faithful will give a satisfactory answer, and will be left to await the Resurrection.

In addition some traditions suggest that the graves of the faithful will be mystically in communion with the *Ka'bah* or the grave of Muhammad, and that in this way they will find comfort and even bliss as they await the resurrection. Those without a satisfactory answer will be beaten continually in the grave until the resurrection. Some traditions excuse the righteous unbelievers from this punishment. Regardless of the specific elaboration of tradition, the primary emphasis is on correct belief as the hope for avoiding immediate punishment in the grave. It is a tradition in Islam that as a person dies he or she whispers the *shahādah*, or basic belief in Allah and Muhammad.

In addition to the hope of avoiding punishment, and finding some comfort in the grave, Islam holds out the possibility of avoiding both the grave and God's final judgment. The prophets are taken directly to paradise upon their death. For ordinary Muslims this privilege is obtained when death comes through martyrdom, primarily when defending Islam. Women who die in childbirth, as well as those who die in the holy land on a pilgrimage, are also martyrs who obtain the entry into paradise directly after death. The hope of a martyr's death has motivated many Muslims to embrace death for Islamic causes. A more benign effect has been to encourage elderly Muslims to put off making their pilgrimage until they are quite feeble, in the hope of dying in the holy land.

## 2. The Judgment Day

Belief in a day of reckoning (*qiyamah*) and a resurrection of the dead to judgment (*hashr*) is found in earliest Islamic creeds, and is universally regarded as an essential doctrine. The earliest revelations to Muhammad stressed the certainty of God's judgment and of punishment in hellfire for wrongdoers and paradise for the righteous. Later revelations and traditions greatly expanded the Islamic picture of the last judgment. None of these revelations offer an absolute assurance of salvation. Indeed to presume to know the judgment of God is itself a sin.

The most basic elements of the Day of Judgment are:

- Signs of the Last Day (the appearance of the Anti-Christ, the descent of Jesus from Heaven, the appearance of the Imam Mahdi, the rise of Gog and Magog, and the rising of the sun from the West).
- The last day when the present creation will be annihilated,
- The resurrection of the dead,
- Their presentation before God and the reading out of the complete record of all their good and evil deeds,

- The rewarding and punishing of each person strictly according to the balance of their good and evil deeds,

- The weighing of good and bad deeds.

- The bridge over which all must pass to enter paradise. This will be knife-edged for sinners, but broad and easy for those who do good. It is generally assumed that there is no intercession for non-Muslims, but some believe that the all the prophets intercede for their followers. It is generally believed that Muhammed intercedes on behalf of sinful Muslims, and that they, after being purged by the fire, will go to paradise. It is also believed by many that the saints can interceded for believers.

- The sending of the successful to paradise, and the losers to the fire and torment of hell.

### 3. Qadā,̄ Qadar

This means literally the will of God and its implementation. Not all creeds list it as a distinct belief, but most Muslims believe that God predestines every person to either heaven or hell. As a doctrine this asserts that nothing happens except that God wills it. This raises the issue of how God can judge people for their actions, since God determines these actions. The most commonly accepted Islamic answer, that of Al-Ash'ari, proposes an understanding similar to Calvinist dual agency. Followers of this school say that humans have the power to convert will into action. But this power does not create anything new, for then it would be beyond the sovereignty of God. Instead they say, "whenever a man desires to do a certain thing, good or bad, the action corresponding to the desire is created by God in his providence. Thus it seems to come from the will of the man, but in fact comes from God." It would be misleading to think that this actually attributes free will to humans, since of course just as God must create the action, so also the intention is predestined, otherwise God's omniscience would not be complete.

### 6. The Unity of Humans with God

From the very beginning of Islam there have been Muslims who sensed a connection between the Oneness of God and the longing of their own

38

souls to be caught up in unity with God. These persons came to be known as *Sufis*, perhaps because the earliest of them wore a distinctive wool garment (*suf* in Arabic) indicating their material poverty and asceticism. Over the ages they became organized into different *tarīqah*. This word indicates both a community and the inner path to unity with the Divine forged by its founder. All the *tarīqah* trace their immediate origin to a teacher whose esoteric knowledge and techniques of meditation form the basis of community life. All claim the ultimate origin of their path is in God, transmitted by the archangel Gabriel to Muhammad and then one of the first companions of the prophet.

## Dhikr

*"And celebrate the name or thy Lord morning and evening, and part of the night, prostrate thyself to Him; and glorify Him a long night through." . . . And part of the night, prostrate thyself to Him; and glorify Him a long night through." (Quran 76:25, 26, 30)*

---

*What makes the Sufi? Purity of heart;*
*Not the patched mantle and the lust perverse*
*Of those vile earth-bound men who steal his name.*
*He in all dregs discerns the essence pure:*
*In hardship ease, in tribulation joy.*
*The phantom sentries, who with batons drawn*
*Guard Beauty's place-gate and curtained bower,*
*Give way before him, unafraid he passes,*
*And showing the King's arrow, enters in.*

*by Rumi, translated by R.A. Nicholson*

---

The starting point for the Sufi's exploration of the esoteric meaning of *tawhīd* is the Quranic injunction to "remember" God as the origin of all that exists and its end. *Dhikr* is the Arabic word for remembrance and it can be used to describe the five pillars of Islam. Yet *dhikr* can mean more than simply calling a fact to consciousness. For the Sufis it means achieving a state of consciousness in which the soul is completely absorbed in the Divine. It is a return to that state prior to self-consciousness in which only consciousness of God exists. In this remembering the self is extinguished (*fanā'*). God's

Oneness is no longer a dogmatic truth held by a person apart from God, but a directly experienced reality. Obedience to God's law, and particularly the keeping of the rituals of daily prayer, fasting, and pilgrimage, is the step toward this goal, but is by no means the last step.

Since the Prophet is regarded as the first Sufi his life, as found in the *Sunnah* (traditions about the Prophet) gives the basic pattern for seeking this Oneness with God the One and only. In that vast corpus of traditions many are suggestive to the Sufis. Muhammad is said to have often spent whole nights in prayer and meditation, as well as reciting the Quran. He frequently fasted. During these times his companions and wives attested to profound external changes that seemed to point to deep shifts in his state of consciousness. Parts of the revelation he received seemed to have a hidden meaning. He is also said to have revealed the esoteric meanings of certain verses to his companions.

The example of the Prophet is expanded upon with techniques that are found in most mystic traditions. Since the prayer rite is the first step in remembrance, it becomes the basis for meditation. Sufis began repeating the basic prayers tens or even hundreds of times as an aid to reaching a state of ecstatic *dhikr*. Different *tarīqah* have different approaches to this. Some focus on the repetition of certain words and phrases from the Quran. For some the physical motions of the prayer rite, repeated again and again, suggest a dance and become one. For others different types of movement such as repeated bowing, dancing in a circle, or spinning like the Mevlevi *dervishes* became part of the ritual. Repeating the name "Allah" in conjunction with deep rhythmic breathing became central to some *dhikr* rituals and was effective in inducing a state of spiritual ecstasy.

In the centuries after Muhammad a rich body of poetry grew up in which the relationship between God and the seeker after unity was compared with that of two lovers. Muhammad's own deep love for his wives, and his manifest sensuality, informed this poetry and became an allegory for the Sufi longing for God. In those *tarīqah* that centered on such a tradition of poetic expression the reading and interpretation of such poems became an important part of the meditative ritual. Setting these poems to music added another dimension to worship in the pursuit of ecstasy. For some Sufis the mystic path was one in which the male and female aspects of being were woven together before being lost in unity. Today the poetry of the greatest mystics, such as Rumi, Hafiz Shirazi, Muhammad Iqbal, and Rabi'a al-Adawiyya, is having a resurgent popularity, even among non-Muslims.

The Unity of All Existence.

As Sufis plunged deeper and deeper into the meaning of both *tawhīd* and their own experience of *fanā'* some became aware of levels of unity that brought them in conflict with conventional Muslim teaching. Ibn Arabi's sentiments could not be shared by many of an exclusivist mind-set.

> *O Marvel! a garden amidst the flames.*
> *My heart has become capable of every form:*
> *it is a pasture for gazelles and a convent for Christian monks,*
> *and a temple for idols and the pilgrim's Ka'bah,*
> *and the tables of the Torah and the book of the Quran.*
> *I follow the religion of Love: whatever way Love's camels take,*
> *that is my religion and my faith.*[12]

Others moved beyond the love as the unifying force behind all religions to see the absolute Oneness of all existence with God, the *wahdat al-wujūd*. Clearly understood, this concept inspired both metaphysical speculation and a large body of literature in many languages. Particularly in the subcontinent and Southeast Asia this idea resonated within cultures already exposed to similar teaching in the *Upanisads* of ancient Vedic religion. Yet taken to logical extremes this concept seemed, at least to some traditional Muslim teachers, nothing other than the sin of *shirk*, or associating creatures as equals with God the creator. Al-Hallaj, a great mystic, and to many saint, once said, "I saw my Lord with the eye of the heart. I said: Who art Thou? He answered: "Thou". Such statements lead him to be condemned and to die a martyr for his belief in *wahdat al-wujūd*.

> *Now stands no more between Truth and me*
> *Or reasoned demonstration,*
> *Or proof of revelation;*
> *Now, brightly blazing full, Truth's illumination*
> *Each flickering, lesser light.*
> *(The last words of Al-Hallaj)*

Not all Sufis, and certainly not all Muslims, would follow al-Hallaj in either his beliefs or his death. Yet all might well look forward to a time when nothing stands between them and the mystery and truth of God's

---

12. Ibn Arabi, as cited by Stephen Hirtenstein, Beshara Magazine, Issue 12, Autumn 1990. Original source cited as: 'Tarjuman al-Ashwaq'. Theosophical Publishing House, 1911. Poem XI.

Oneness. Not all Muslims are Sufis, and yet all hope to say as they die, "There is no God but God."

## Guide for Further Study

Review the key themes of the chapter. If members of the study group have questions about these key themes it would be good to discuss them first.

### Key Themes

- There is no god besides God/Allah.

- Monotheism is the fundamental human religion, taught through prophets in every culture and age.

- God can be known by examining the created order and listening when God speaks to the human heart.

- God predetermines all things, and humans must submit (the meaning of "Islam") to God's will.

- *Shirk*, or making anyone or thing equal to God, is the worst possible sin.

- Muslim mystics (Sufis) seek an experience of completely merging with God's being through meditation, ritual prayer, and esoteric knowledge.

- Since the final revelation of the Quran there should be only one religion (Islam) and one community (*ummah*).

- The religion of Islam consists of five fundamental religious obligations and five or six fundamental beliefs.

  - The five religious obligations are: 1. the declaration of faith (*shahādah*), 2. the five daily prayers, 3. the fasting month, 4. the pilgrimage to Mecca (*hajj*), and 5. the religious tax/almsgiving (*zakāt*).

  - The five beliefs are: 1. the oneness of God, 2. the existence of angels, 3. the different books of revelation, culminating in the Quran, 4. the prophets of God, Muhammad being the last, 5. God's final judgment of humanity, and with that the acceptance of God's predestination of all persons to either paradise or hell.

Questions for Discussion

- Christians believe that God is one, yet within God's being there is a dynamism expressed by the idea that God is also Trinity: Father, Son, and Holy Spirit. How would you explain this to a Muslim?

- Muslims believe that God is both immanent and transcendent. Is Christian belief different? How?

- Christians also believe in the ideal of a single faith and a single community of faith. How is the Christian ideal different from that of Islam?

- How do Christian beliefs differ from those of Muslims regarding God's prophets and the scriptures?

- How do your beliefs about death and the final judgment differ from those of Muslims?

- How do Christians "remember" that they come from, and return to, God?

Additional Readings

The following readings are from a prominent Nigerian Muslim theologian, as well as Sayyed Hossein Nasr, whose work is mentioned in chapter 1. Selections from the Quran follow. As you read, ask yourself whether the concept of God's oneness plays the same role in Islam as in Christianity.

Idris, Jafaar Sheik. "Tawhīd." In *Faces of Islam*, edited by Zaiuddin Sardar and Merryl Wyn Davies. Kuala Lumpur, Malaysia: Beritang, 1989.

Excerpts from Chapter 1 (All quotations from the Quran are as found in the original text.)

1. The word *Tawhīd* comes from the Arabic word *Wahid*, or *ahad*, which means one, and it refers to what is for us the most fundamental, the most important fact that is that there is only one God. *Tawhīd* has three aspects: we acknowledge the fact that it is this God who creates, who sustains everything, who preserves the world. This much is acknowledged by many people, whether they be Muslims or non-Muslims . . . The other aspect is that this God has attributes that are very unique,

attributes that are not shared by anything else. That doesn't mean that we don't say, for example, that "God knows." But rather it means that when this attribute applies to God it applies to Him in a way in which it does not apply to human beings. The third aspect which the most important is that it is only this God who deserves to be worshipped. . . . *"La ilaha illal Lah"* is the basic tenet of belief whose real meaning is that there is no God worthy of being worshipped except the one true God who we call in Arabic, Allah.

Quran 43:82, *Holy is Allah, the Lord of the heavens and the earth, the Lord of the Throne, far above that which they attribute to Him.*

Quran 2:255 *Allah—there is no god save Him, the Living, the Self-Subsisting and All-Sustaining. Slumber seizes Him not, nor sleep. To Him belongs whatsoever is in the heavens and whatsoever is in the earth. Who is he that dare intercede with Him save by HIS permission? He knows what is before them and what is behind them; and they encompass nothing of HIS knowledge, except what He pleases. HIS knowledge extends over the heavens and the earth; and the care of them wearies Him not; and He is the High, the Great.*

2. *Tawhīd* is like the premise from which all the details of Islam are deduced, everything in Islam is related to *tawhīd*. Because according to Islam every human being is born a Muslim so *tawhīd* is the essence of human being. Every human being is born with *tawhīd* and when he deviates from *tawhīd* he is alienated. If he becomes a Muslim in fact he returns to the religion of his human nature, he becomes himself. And this *tawhīd* is linked with the best that is in human beings.

## Additional Question

- Idris stresses that all of Islam derives from the *Oneness* of God. What would you say is the central fact about God from which Christian faith springs?

Nasr, Seyyed Hossein. "God." In *Islamic Spirituality*, edited by Seyyed Hossein Nasr, vol. 1. New York: The Crossroad, 1987.

Excerpts from Chapter 16

1. The Quranic verse "He IS THE FIRST and the Last, the Outward and the Inward" (57:3) refers not only to the Divine Nature but also to God's role and function in Islamic spirituality, for God is alpha and omega of Islamic spirituality and both its inner and outer reality. He is at the center of the arena of Islamic life, and all facets and dimensions of spirituality revolve around Him, seek Him, and are concerned with Him as the goal of human existence. (p. 311)

2. The Quran is like one long melody whose refrain is the Divine Oneness for God is at once One in Himself (*al-ahad*) and One with respect to His creation (*al-wahid*). (p. 313)

3. Precisely because God is at once absolute and infinite, the Divine Nature, although usually referred to in the masculine, also possess a feminine "aspect," which is, in fact, the principle of all femininity. If God in His absoluteness and majesty is the Origin of the masculine principle, in His Infinitude and beauty God is the Origin of femininity. Moreover, if as Creator and Judge God is seen in Islam as He, the Sufis point out that as Mercy and Forgiveness God can be envisaged and symbolized as the Beloved or the female who is the object of the spiritual guest. The Divine Compassion, *al-Rahmah*, is grammatically feminine in Arabic, as in the Divine Essence *(al-Dhar)* Itself, so that femininity symbolizes the aspect of inwardness beauty, and mercy of the Divine. (p. 316)

4. God also penetrates His creation though His "signs" (*āyāt*) which are manifested both in the world of nature and within the soul man, for the Quran asserts, "We shall display to them our signs (*āyāt*) upon the horizons (*afaq*) and within themselves (*anfus*) until it becomes manifest to them that it is the truth (*al-haqq*)"(41, 53) . . . God has left His "signature" upon all things in a language whose key is provided by Revelation. (p. 320)

5. As far as Islamic spirituality is concerned, the aspect of God as Love and also as Light are particularly significant and have led to distinct modes of spirituality . . . Moreover, one of God's Names is *al Wadud*, He Who loves, and Sufis usually refer to the Divine as the object of

love. . . . The Quran states that "God is the Light *(nūr)* of the heavens and the earth" (24:35). Therefore, all light issues from His Light, from the physical light of the candle to the light of the sun and even beyond to the angelic and archangelic lights which illuminate the soul. (p. 321)

## Additional Questions

- Nasr emphasizes that God and the Oneness of God is the center of Islamic spirituality. How is this different from your understanding of the center of Christian spirituality?

- Nasr emphasizes that God embraces both masculine and feminine qualities. What would you regard as the masculine and feminine aspects of the Christian understanding of God?

- The Divine Names, or the ninety-nine names of Allah, play an important role in Muslim spirituality. What names for God play an important role in Christian spirituality? How do we use different names and titles for God and Jesus in our worship and prayer?

## Other Readings from the Quran on God

28:88 *And call not, besides Allah, on another god. There is no god but He. Everything (that exists) will perish except His Face. To Him belongs the Command, and to Him will ye (all) be brought back.*

57:1–4 *Whatever is in the heavens and on earth, declares the Praises and Glory of Allah: for He is the Exalted in Might, the Wise. To Him belongs the dominion of the heavens and the earth: it is He Who gives Life and Death; and He has Power over all things. He is the First and the Last, the Evident and the Hidden: and He has full knowledge of all things. He it is Who created the heavens and the earth in six Days, then established Himself on the Throne. He knows what enters within the earth and what comes forth out of it, what comes down from heaven and what mounts up to it. And He is with you wheresoever ye may be. And Allah sees well all that ye do.*

20:14 *Verily, I am Allah. There is no god but I: So serve thou Me (only), and establish regular prayer for My remembrance.*

112:1–4 *Say: He is Allah, the One; Allah, the Eternal, Absolute; He begetteth not, nor is He begotten; And there is none like unto Him*

24:35 *God is the Light.*

Additional Questions

- Muslims speak of God as love and light, both of which are revealed in creation. What is the key revelation of God's love and light for Christians?

- Muslims associate the sentences (āyāt) of the Quran with the signs (āyāt) of God in creation. What is, for Christians, God's sign and God's Word?

The poems below belong to a long tradition of Muslim poetry which extols God's unity, and what it means for our humanity. Particularly in the Sufi tradition poetry rather than philosophical speculation has been seen as the best means to grasp and experience a concept that cannot be conceived with mere rationality.

Al Hallaj (CE 858–922). "Before does not outstrip Him." In *The Doctrine of the Sufis* by A. J. Arberry. Lahore: Sh. Muhammad Ashraf Lahore, 1966.

> *"Before" does not outstrip Him,*
>
> *"after" does not interrupt Him*
>
> *"of" does not vie with Him for precedence*
>
> *"from" does not accord with Him*
>
> *"to" does not join with Him*
>
> *"in" does not inhabit Him*
>
> *"when" does not stop Him*
>
> *"if" does not consult with Him*
>
> *"over" does not overshadow Him*
>
> *"under" does not support Him*
>
> *"opposite" does not face Him*
>
> *"with" does not press Him*
>
> *"behind" does not limit Him*
>
> *"previous" does not display Him*
>
> *"after" does not cause Him to pass away*

*"all" does not unite Him*

*"is" does not bring Him into being*

*"is not" does not deprive Him from Being.*

*Concealment does not veil Him*

*His pre-existence preceded time,*

*His being preceded non-being,*

*His eternity preceded limit.*

*If thou sayest 'when,' His existing has outstripped time;*

*If thou sayest 'before,' before is after Him;*

*If thou sayest 'he,' 'h' and 'e' are His creation;*

*If thou sayest 'how,' His essence is veiled from description;*

*If thou sayest 'where,' His being preceded space;*

*If thou sayest 'ipseity' (ma huwa), His ipseity (huwiwah) is*

*apart from things.*

*Other than He cannot be qualified by two (opposite) qualities at*

*one time; yet With Him they do not create opposition.*

*He is hidden in His manifestation, manifest in His concealing.*

*He is outward and inward, near and far; and in this respect He is*

*removed beyond the resemblance of creation.*

*He acts without contact,*

*instructs without meeting,*

*guides without pointing.*

*Desires do not conflict with Him,*

*thoughts do not mingle with Him:*

*His essence is without qualification (takyeef),*

*His action without effort (takleef).*

Yunus Emri. "I am a fatherless pearl unrecognized by the sea." In *The Drop that Became the Sea*, translated by Refik Algan and Edmund Helminski. Vermont: Threshold, 1989. Quoted at: http://www.khamush.com/sufism/yunus_emre.htm

> *I am a fatherless pearl unrecognized by the sea.*
> *I am the drop that contains the ocean.*
>
> *Its waves are amazing. It's beautiful to be a sea*
> *hidden within an infinity drop.*
>
> *When Majnun spoke Layla's name,*
> *he broke the meter of his poem.*
> *I was both Layla and Majnun who adored her.*
>
> *Mansur did not speak idly of Unity.*
> *He was not kidding when he said, "I am Truth."*
>
> *In this world of many,*
> *You are Joseph and I am Jacob.*
> *In the universe of Unity,*
> *there is neither Joseph nor Canaan.*
>
> *That my name is Yunus*
> *is a problem in this material world.*
> *But if you ask my real name*
> *it is the Power behind all powers.*

## Further Question

- Muslim mystics have traditionally used poetry both to express their insights into God's essence, and their desire to be one with God. How are these poems similar to Christian hymns, poems, and songs that you know?

# Chapter 3: Muhammad

"And Muhammad is his Prophet." The first pillar of Islam is an affirmation of faith, "There is no God but Allah, and Muhammad is his Prophet." It should remind us of the indivisibility of the core message of Islam and the messenger Muhammad in the hearts and minds of Muslims. This does not mean that all Muslims see Muhammad in the same way. It does mean that any account of his life not refracted through the eyes of faith will fall short of Muslim expectations.

## 1. Muhammad's Life

*Time Line of Muhammad's Life*

*571: Birth of the Prophet Muhammad.*

*583: The Prophet's journey to Syria in the company of his uncle Abu Talib. His meeting with the monk Bahira at Bisra who foretells of his prophethood.*

*594: The Prophet becomes the business manager of Khadija and leads her trade caravan to Syria and back.*

*595: The Prophet marries Hadrat Khadija.*

*605: The Prophet arbitrates in a dispute among the Quraish about the placing of the Black Stone in the Kaaba.*

*610: The first revelation in the cave at Mt. Hira.*

*613: Declaration at Mt. Sara inviting the general public to Islam.*

*615: Persecution of the Muslims by the Quraish. A party of Muslims leaves for Abyssinia.*

*617: Social boycott of the Hashimites and the Prophet by the Quraish.*

*619: Lifting of the boycott. Deaths of Abu Talib and Hadrat Khadija. Year of sorrow.*

*620: Journey to Taif. Ascension to the heavens.*

Muhammad was born in Mecca, into the Quraysh tribe, around 570 CE. His early life was spent under the guardianship of first his paternal grandfather and then his uncle Abu Talib, whom he accompanied on trading journeys into Syria. Around 596 on one such journey he was caring for the merchandise of a wealthy Meccan woman named Khatijah, of the Asad clan. Impressed by his honestly and skill, she offered to marry him. Although she was already forty years old, they later had six children together, two sons who died young and four daughters.

From 610 until his death in 632 Muhammad periodically had visions of God's greatness and majesty, and received a series of revelations that would first be gathered together into the Quran in 650. Muhammad was at first stunned and scared by his visions and revelations. Then with the sympathetic support of his wife he began to accept his role of God's Prophet and messenger. In 613 he began preaching publicly, and immediately attracted followers of his message emphasizing the oneness and majesty of God and the certainty of his judgment against those who violate the Divine law. He also rapidly attracted opposition to a message that struck at many basic practices and beliefs of the Arab tribes in Mecca. In 619 when his wife and uncle died, he found himself without close allies against the more powerful leaders in Mecca. Facing physical threats and psychological harassment, Muhammad began negotiating with the tribes occupying Yathrib, an oasis to the north, and in 622 he and his followers made the *hijrah* or migration to this new center. There they formed a ninth "tribe" in confederation with the eight already there.

In the next several years the followers of Muhammad engaged in raids against Meccan caravans, gradually gaining strength and prestige. They also attracted enemies in Medina, including some from among Muhammad's followers and the Jewish clan that ran the market. These enemies of the Prophet were expelled from Medina in 625. Two years later there was a second conflict in Medina. When the Jewish clan opposing

Muhammad surrendered after the battle, Muhammad had them put to the sword. Having established his power in Medina, Muhammad effectively governed Yathrib, which became known as the "city of the Prophet" or just Medina, "the city."

---

*Timeline of Muhammad's Life, continued*

*622: The Prophet and the Muslims migrate to Yathrib.*

*624: Battle of Badr. Expulsion of the Bani Qainuqa Jews from Md-dina.*

*625: Battle of Uhud. Massacre of seventy Muslims at Bir Mauna. Expulsion of Banu Nadir Jews from Madina. Second expedition of Badr.*

*627: Battle of the Trench. Expulsion of Banu Quraiza Jews.*

*629: The Prophet performs the pilgrimage at Mecca.*

*630: Conquest of Mecca.*

*632: Farewell pilgrimage at Mecca.*

*632: Death of the Prophet. Election of Hadrat Abu Bakr as the Caliph. Usamah leads expedition to Syria.*

---

From this point forward Muhammad used a combination of persuasion and economic pressure (through raids on caravans) to win the Meccan tribes to Islam. In 629 he and his followers made a pilgrimage to Mecca. In January 630 Muhammad responded to Meccan attacks on the Muslims by launching an expedition against Mecca with over 10,000 men. He entered the city with almost no resistance, and soon large numbers of Meccans converted to the new religion. Among the Arab tribes many soon followed suit. At a battle later in the year the nomadic tribes joined against Muhammad were defeated, and in the next year the Arabs were united as followers of Muhammad. In 632 he led a second pilgrimage to Mecca. Later in the same year he died.

No brief account of Muhammad's life can convey the admiration his contemporaries had for his character. He was known, both as general and administrator, as a man of courage, impartiality, and generosity. Men and women found him personally charming. He alternated between periods of deep silence, introspection, and meditation and those of vigorous activity. To his followers this simply demonstrated his virtues as both a man of faith and a man of action. In time their regard for him would grow. He would be regarded not only as the founder of a state and a religion, but as: 1) a source of Muslim hope for salvation 2) a source for the Muslim way of life, as 3) the font of a meaningful life and 4) as the mystic path that leads to union with God.

## 2. Muhammad as the Touchstone of the Muslim Hope

The beginning of Muslim devotion to Muhammad is the constant repetition of the *tasliya*, or blessing of the Prophet. In print it is indicated by "s.a.w." from the words of the blessing in Arabic or "pbuh" from "praise be upon him" in English. It is the single most common phrase in Muslim devotions, and is the ending of virtually every Muslim prayer. Early in Muslim history it became an essential part of a life of salvation and devotion to God. Now it is heard at the end of every call to prayer, and is a repeated refrain within the ritual of five times daily prayer. Nor is this merely a matter of obedient devotion. For Muslims it is a part of their hope in this life and the next. An important tradition says the Muhammad himself promised that, "whoso calls down one blessing on me, God shall call down on him ten blessings."[1]

The promised benefits of blessing the Prophet begin with death. Muslims believe that the soul is in some way sensible in the grave during the period between death and the final judgment. For non-Muslims this is a time of punishment and torture for their failure to believe. Even for Muslims the thought of a lonely existence in the grave, however peaceful, can be terrifying. They have the promise, however, that blessing the Prophet "widens the narrowness of the tomb and solaces for me its loneliness." It can even become a pleasant and spacious garden for those who have blessed Muhammad, or a path to communion with the Prophet in his tomb.[2]

Beyond the promise of solace in the grave there is the assurance that those who bless the Prophet will be saved from punishment for their sins. A tradition states that Ubayy bin Ka'b told Muhammad, "I will devote my whole prayer to you." The Prophet replied, "Then your anxieties will be met

1. Muslim and Siddiqi, *Sahih Muslim.*
2. Padwick, *Muslim Devotions,* 161.

and your sins forgiven."[3] Many other traditions confirm that calling down a blessing on the Prophet is the best of all works, and overcomes a multitude of sins, broadening the way into paradise after the final judgment. One tradition reports that Muhammad said:

> "When a man is ordered to the Fire I shall say, 'bring him back to the scales (place of judgment),' and I shall add to the scale (of his good deeds) something small as a finger tip, and that is his calling down of blessing on me. And the scale will be balanced and the cry will go up, 'happy is so and so.'"[4]

Within this life devotion to the Prophet becomes a path of communion with God. Prayer manuals tell the Muslim that God and God's angels call down blessings on Muhammad, and thus the Muslim who does the same participates in part of the life of the heavenly community at prayer.[5] This can also be seen as a communion of love, joining in *the calling down of the blessing by the Beloved on his beloved.*[6] In this way the blessing of the Prophet that all Muslims call down in their daily prayers becomes, as discussed below, an important part of the spiritual path to inner transformation, and for the mystics the path toward oneness with the divine.

## 3. Muhammad's Life as the Muslim Way of Life

> *It is on this basis that we assert with full knowledge and conviction and without any prejudice that of all the Prophets (pbuh) and religious leaders, it is the Prophet Muhammad (pbuh) alone to whom humanity can turn for advice and guidance . . .*
>
> Mawdudi, in *The Message of the Prophet's Seerat*

The lifelong participation in devotion to the Prophet, with its attendant promises, gives Muhammad a place in the Muslim heart that makes any attack on his character or status as God's last voice among humankind deeply offensive. It is an attack on the foundations of human faith and hope. At the

3. Ibid, 155.

4. Ibid, 161.

5. Much like the Christian who, during the Eucharist, participates in the worship with "angels and archangels and all the company of heaven."

6. Padwick, *Muslim Devotions*, 157.

same time Muhammad's life becomes, in Islam, the basic guide and justi-fication for almost every action. For Christians the question, "What would Jesus do?" is most often the starting point for reflection on the character of Jesus, and how it would be realized in the modern world. For Muslims the question "What would Muhammad do?" is answered far more concretely with literally hundreds of accounts relating the Prophet's actions and words in a vast range of human situations (*hadith*).

These accounts are found in numerous collections of varying antiquity. Together they comprise the *Sunnah* (tradition) of the Prophet: the touch-stone for ordering every aspect of life and the most common currency of daily conversation. They are also a fundamental source of Islamic law. And, of course each reference to the *Sunnah* of Muhammad reinforces his honor and esteem. No Muslim would refer to Muhammad's words without adding, "praise be upon him," calling down the blessing once again.

If a child wonders why he dresses in a certain way the answer will be that Muhammad (praise be upon him) dressed in this way. If she wonders why she must keep her promises under any circumstances it will be because Muhammad (praise be upon him) said, *"He who is not trustworthy has no Faith, and he who does not keep his Covenant has no religion."* If there is a question about the value of schooling, a parent may well answer, *"He who goes out in search of knowledge is in God's path till he returns."* To the person who acts in anger or haste there may come the Prophet's rebuke, *"You have two characters which God likes: gentleness and deliberation."* And should the believer wonder why all this attention is paid to the Prophet, then Muham-mad himself (praise be upon him) provides the answer: *"None of you believes till I am dearer to him than his father, his child and all mankind."*[7]

The traditions of the Prophet are also the means by which disputes are resolved in matters of both faith and practice, and are thus fundamental to Muslim apologetics. If a non-Muslim accuses Islam of oppressing women the Muslim will frequently reply with a quotation from the farewell speech of Muhammad, *"Do treat your women well and be kind to them for they are your partners and committed helpers."* If prejudice arises in the Muslim com-munity, those who show it will be reminded that in the same sermon Mu-hammad said, *"All mankind is from Adam and Eve, an Arab has no superiority over a non-Arab nor a non-Arab has any superiority over an Arab; also a white*

7. All the Hadith in this chapter are found in the collections of Baihaqi, Tarimi, Mus-lim, and Bukari. The original source is published by the Muslim Student Association, University of Southern California, no date; located at http://www.usc.edu/dept/MSA/fundamentals/hadithsunnah/muslim/.

*has no superiority over a black nor a black has any superiority over a white—except by piety and good action. Learn that every Muslim is a brother to every Muslim and that the Muslims constitute one brotherhood."*

In addition to the repetition of the traditions to address every human and social need, Muslims are taught to love the Prophet through constant exposure to the *sirat* (plural of *sirah*), or stories of his life and that of his wives and relatives. The *sirah* of Ibn Ishaq is one of the earliest and a standard source of later biographies. It tells not only of what the Prophet did and said, but also alludes to miracles surrounding his birth and signs that accompanied his life and deeds. Many of these are related in several forms, drawn from collections of traditions. In later *sirat* the miraculous and nearly superhuman aspects of Muhammad's character and religious experience are even more pronounced. In no *sirat* to which Muslims are regularly exposed is the Prophet's character or actions subject to critique. And when they run contrary to either modern standards of behavior or even the Prophet's own teaching, they are inevitably not only justified, but praised.[8] Thus the apparent contradiction between the Prophet's sexual life and his ascetic life is said to be "in reality a positive bi-polarity" which reflects the movement of the soul in various stages toward God.[9]

## 4. Muhammad as the Epitome of Meaningful Life

When we consider this constant, and highly idealized, presence of Muhammad's life and words in Muslim life, we can understand how central his character is to Muslim faith. To treat Muhammad with less than utmost respect is to challenge directly the value of Islam. To attack Muhammad is to attack every Muslim life: to challenge its authenticity, and to question its worth.

This can be seen in two events of the last decade. The first, well known, was the death warrant declared by the Ayatollah Khomeini on Salman Rushdie for his book *The Satanic Verses*. In his book Rushdie made remarks that appeared to disparage Muhammad and the book was quickly banned

8. "The Life of the Prophet" by Ja'far Qasimi in Nasr, ed., *Islamic Spirituality*, a work in English for a non-Muslim audience, is an excellent example. Muhammad's marriage to an under-aged female relative, his voracious sexual appetite, his keeping of slaves, and fundamental disagreements between Shi' and Sunni Muslim over his last days are passed by without critical comment.

9. Nasr, ed., *Islamic Spirituality*, 59.

in virtually every Muslim country. Even defenders of Rushdie's artistic freedom came under attack, and two translators of the book were killed. Rushdie himself went into hiding for nearly a decade.

More telling in terms of the value placed upon the *Sunnah* of the Prophet has been the suppression of any Muslim movement that asserts that the Quran alone should be the source of Islamic law and belief. In the late 1980s and 1990s a group in Malaysia known as the *Jemaah Al Quran*, led at one time by Kassim Ahmad, asserted that the *hadith* (the traditional sayings of Muhammad) should not be used in determining questions of Muslim belief and practice. This movement, which seems so much like the Reformation in Christianity, was outlawed. Ahmad's book *The Hadith: A New Evaluation* was banned, and many members of the *Jemaah Al Quran* were hounded out of their positions in the government and academia.

As importantly, this movement found no public defenders among either intellectuals or those with political power. Similar attacks have been launched against the followers of Rashid Khalifa, who has promoted similar ideas in the Arab and European Muslim worlds. The Ahmadiyya movement, whose founder Hazrat Mirza Ghulam questioned the role of the Hadith, has likewise been outlawed or suppressed in much of the Muslim world. The ferocity directed at those who attack Muhammad, or who appear to devalue of his words and works, demonstrates how foundational they are to faith, and the confidence of Muslims that lives built on the life of Muhammad are lives in the way of God.

### 5. Muhammad as the Mystic Way

The enlargement of the character of Muhammad after his death didn't just relate to his excellence in personal virtue, leadership of the community in peace and war, and his roles as husband and father. Muhammad as the bearer of God's revelation is also the key to navigating the way from God to the world, and from the world to God. Hidden in Muhammad's life is the substance of prophecy: the soul of the human being that God used to make Godself known to humanity. As Hussein Nasr says,

> *"If love of God can be said to lie at the center of the spiritual life, it must be asserted that no one can love God unless God loves him, and God loves only the person who loves his Prophet. Since the love of the Prophet is, therefore, the secret key for the unlocking of the gates that open into the Divine presence, it is an essential part of Islamic*

*spirituality . . . The Prophet is the infallible guide and the source of*
*all spiritual guidance in Islam; and his Sirah, Sunnah, and hadith*
*constitute the ship that carries those who aspire to the spiritual life*
*across the waters of earthly existence to the shore of that land which*
*bathes in the Divine Presence."*[10]

For the mystic this means not only a literal obedience to the example of the
Prophet. It means finding the inner meaning of the Prophet's life grasped
through an esoteric interpretation of its outward forms. Frithjof Schuon,
a European Sufi, explains that beyond the Prophet as a human man, the
mystic must see the Prophetic "Substance," which "represents esotericism at
every level." The *Sunnah* of the Prophet is, at a non-literal level, the "Moham-
medan Substance" through which the mystic can approach God and enjoy
complete communion with God such as the Prophet himself had. Through
the *Sunnah*, understood using symbolic and numerological systems of interpretation, the Prophet is *immanent* to his followers today, and can thus
inculcate in *them* the beauty and serenity of soul which he inculcated in his
original followers. Thus, for Schuon the Prophet is the Logos who eternally
makes communion with God a possibility.[11] There is a *barakah* or blessing
that is more than just a concrete reward for obedience. It is an atmosphere
of Divine presence found in both persons and places that are in conformity
and close communion with this "Substance."

An example of this kind of mystical interpretation of the tradition of
the Prophet is found in the Sufi interpretation of the meaning of a tradition that says, "Women, perfumes, and prayer were made lovable to the
Prophet." For the mystic, "women" symbolizes the extinction of self and
total unity with the Being of God, and the generosity or "self-giving" which
makes this possible. "Perfumes" symbolize freshness, harmony, and equi-
librium, and a general sense of the divine in an ambiance, as emanation,
or as an aura. And prayer is not only a verbal act, it is an inward "remembrance" of God and thus a giving of the self to God out of love. Thus, *"In*
*speaking of women Muhammad is essentially speaking of his inward nature;*
*in speaking of perfumes he has in mind the world around us, the ambience;*
*and in speaking of prayer, he is giving expression to his love of God."*[12] Such a
symbolic interpretation of a single tradition of the Prophet can be carried

10. Ibid, 64.

11. Ibid, 48.

12. Ibid, 59.

58

out on many others, as on the verses of the Quran, to yield a rich account of the journey of the soul toward God.

## 6. The Family of the Prophet

*Abu Humaid Al-Sa'idi, may Allah be pleased with him, reported:*

*"They (the Companions of the Holy Prophet) asked: Messenger of Allah, how should we pray for you? He (the Holy Prophet) observed: Say: 'O Allah! Bless Muhammad, his wives and his off-spring, as You did bless the family of Abraham, and grant favors to Muhammad, his wives and his offspring, as You did grant favors to the family of Abraham; You are Praiseworthy and Glorious.'"*

*(Sahih Muslim 615)*

In popular Muslim piety the honor and respect shown the family of Muhammad continues to provide a concrete, personal means of honoring the Prophet himself. Those who claim descent from Muhammad often use the title *sayyid* or *sayyed*, (which can be used as a more general honorific as well) or they will indicate their descent from the Prophet with *sharif* in their name. They are also referred to as the *mawley* in the Arab west. Muslims usually honor them by kissing their hand, placing their hand against the forehead, or in other ways appropriate to the particular culture seeking a blessing. In Southeast Asia and the subcontinent the *shurafa* (plural of *sharif*) are a valued symbol of continuity with the original Muslim community, and often are looked to for leadership in religious matters.

## 7. Conclusion

For the mystic the assimilation of the "Prophetic Substance" and thus One-ness with God is the ultimate goal of Islam. For every Muslim the assimilation of the Prophet's way of life into his or her own life through imitation fulfills the ultimate goal of total submission to God. Islam as a way of life and the Prophet are thus inseparable, and the Prophet is in every respect an ideal that both motivates and encourages the Muslim to a deeper life of faith. In this respect Islam, like Christianity, can never be reduced to either dogma or metaphysics, but will always have a human face at its center.

## Guide for Further Study

Review the key themes of the chapter. If members of the study group have questions about these key themes it would be good to discuss them first.

### Key Themes

- Muhammad lived between 570 and 632 CE. He received his revelations between 610 and 632, and ruled a growing Muslim community from 613 onward.

- In 622 the Muslim community moved to Medina (hijrah), and in 630 Muhammad and his followers were able to take control of Mecca. By the time of Muhammad's death all the Arab tribes had become Muslim, and Muslim armies controlled the Arabian Peninsula and parts of modern Iraq, Syria, and Persia.

- Blessing the Prophet is a requirement for Muslims. Moreover it is a means by which they are forgiven their failings and receive hope for a blessed existence after death and before the final judgment.

- Up to today Muslims honor and bless the descendants of the Prophet as a way of obtaining God's blessings on their lives.

- For Sufis love of the Prophet, esoteric interpretation of his words, and imitation of his meditative practices, are the ways in which they can mystically join in the "Prophetic Substance" and enjoy the oneness with God which he enjoyed.

- Muhammad is the primary example for how Muslims should live.

- Muhammad's words and actions are the sunnah (tradition) of the Prophet and are contained in collections of hadith, or accounts of individual sayings and acts.

- The sunnah is, next to the Quran, the fundamental guide for living a Muslim life. All Muslims seek to imitate Muhammad.

### Questions for Discussion

- Given the brief account of Muhammad's life, what makes it difficult for Christians to see him as a spiritual leader?

- In what ways is Muhammad's role like, and unlike, that of Jesus?

- Muslims believe that blessing the Prophet will give them peace in the grave. What do Christians believe gives them hope of peace and blessedness between the time they die and the final judgment?

- Muslims often say that they are more respectful of Jesus as a prophet than Christians are of Jesus. How do Christians indicate their respect for Jesus and why is it different from that of Muslims?

- Muslim mystics speak about the "Prophetic Substance" as the key characteristic of Muhammad's life that linked him with God, and which they hope will link them with God. Christians speak of the "Spirit of Christ" or "Holy Spirit," which draws them into oneness with God. Are there similarities with Islamic ideas?

## Additional Readings

The readings below come from Seyyed Hossein Nasr, who relates the traditional love and esteem of Muslims for the Prophet, followed by a critical evaluation of just the literature that encourages such devotion. The readings from the Quran are a different source of Muslim spirituality, which finds a place for both Jesus and Muhammad.

**Nasr, Seyyed Hossein. "Sunnah and Hadith." In** *Islamic Spirituality,* **edited by Seyyed Hossein Nasr, vol. 1. New York: Crossroad, 1987.**

### Excerpts from Chapter 5, part II

1. The perfection inherent in the Prophet as God's most noble and perfect creature could not but manifest itself in his physical features. He was said to possess an exceptionally beautiful countenance, which has been extolled over the ages. . . .

. . . In the Muslim eye, this appreciation of the beauty of the Prophet is directly related to the love for him and constitutes a basic aspect of Islamic spirituality complementing the fear, love, and knowledge of God, the One who is at once transcendent and immanent.

. . . The chanting of the litanies of the names of the Prophet is an important practice in Sufism and on a more external level in the everyday activity of many pious Muslims. The Turkish Sufi poet Yunis Emre sang seven centuries ago:

> *Please pray for us on Doomsday Thy name is beautiful, thou thyself art beautiful, Muhammad! Thy words are accepted near God, the Lord Thy name is beautiful, thou thyself art beautiful.*

Not only is the Prophet called Muhammad, the most praised one, but he is also *Ahmad,* the most praiseworthy of those who praise God. He is *Wahid,* the unique one; *Mat,* the annihilator of darkness and ignorance; and *'Aqib* the last of the prophets. He is *Tahir,* the pure and clean one; *Tayyib* ,he who possesses beauty and fragrance; and *Sayyid,* prince and master of the universe. He is, of course, *Rasul,* messenger, but also *Rasul alRahmah,* the messenger of mercy; and *Khatim alrusul,* the seal of prophets. He is *'Abd Allah,* the perfect servant of God, but also *Habib Allah,* the beloved of God; and *Safi Allah,* the one chosen by God. He is both *Nasir,* the victorious helper of men, and *Mansur,* the one who is made triumphant in this world.

The Prophet is *Muhyi,* the vivifier of the dead hearts of men, and *Munji,* he who delivers man from sin. He is *Nūr,* light, as well as *Siraj,* the torch that illuminates the path in man's life; *Misbah,* the lamp that contains the light of faith; and *Huda,* the guide to God and paradise. He is *Dhu quwwah,* the possessor of strength; *Dhu hurmah,* possessor of sacred reverence; and *Dhu makanah,* the possessor of integrity. He is both *Amin,* trustworthy, and *Sadiq,* truthful. He is the *Miftah* or key to paradise, and *Miftah alrahmah,* the key to God's Mercy. The love of the Prophet is in fact both a sign of the love of God and the gate to that Mercy from which the very substance of the universe was created. (pp.98–100)

## Additional Questions

- For Muslims Muhammad is the "perfect man" and the example of every human virtue and beauty. He is, however, only a man and a prophet. How is this different from the Christian conception of Jesus? How does this make the Islamic concept of humanity different from that of Christianity?

- For Muslims the Quran is God's final and complete revelation, and Muhammad is the final prophet. If Jesus is God's Word, does the revelation of God in Christ end with his death?

- Muslims frequently describe the physical beauty of Muhammad but are reluctant to show any picture of his face for fear of slipping into idolatry. Does Christian spirituality depend on descriptions or pictures of Jesus?

Sardar Zaiuddin, *Islamic Futures*. Petaling Jaya, Malaysia: Pelanduk, 1988.

Excerpts from Part 2, Chapter 11

1. The Sirah, the life of the Beloved Prophet Mohammad, has to be made more meaningful and significant to Muslim individuals and societies. (p. 241)

2. The Sirah literature is a unique institution of Islam. Sirah, the life of the Prophet Mohammed, is both history and biography. But more than that: it is a source of guidance as well as of law. It is in the Sirah that Muslims seek inspiration of their behavior and understanding of the Quran. As much, the Sirah is an integral part of the Shariah or Islamic law. Thus the Sirah is biography, history, law and guidance all integrated together. It therefore transcends time and has eternal value as a model of ideal Muslim behaviour and a practical demonstration of the eternal principles and injunctions of the Quran. (p. 242)

3. The classical Sirah literature, cast as it is in an idiom which is over 1,200 years old, does not have the same impact on a modern mind as it had on the early Muslims. . . . Unfortunately, modern authors for some strange but compelling reason, have stuck to the classical method of writing the Sirah. The result is that the life of Mohammad, which is the paradigm of Muslim behaviour, *uswa hasna*, makes no real sense to the vast majority of contemporary Muslims. (p. 244)

4. What is important about the Sirah of the Prophet Mohammad are the causes and principles for which the Prophet lived and the operational form he gave to the basic concepts and ideas of Islam. The Muslims are not obliged to do, even if it was possible, what the Prophet did. But they are required to promote the norms of behavior and the principles of life which are the *raison d'etre* of the Sirah. Only studies of the Sirah from the perspective of ideas and concepts, seeking to answer the questions of why and how, can turn the life of Mohammad into a living reality. And only by turning the Sirah from a historical narrative

into a contemporary map of guidance can Muslims fully appreciate the future significance of the life of Mohammad. (p. 255)

## Additional Questions

- In the Bible we read about several different types of religious leaders: seers, prophets, priests, teachers/rabbis, scribes, Pharisees, and others. Often, as in the case of Moses or Saul a religious leader was also a political or military leader as well. With which of the religious leaders found in the Bible would you compare Muhammad?

- Zaiuddin Sadar calls for Muslims to write critical and relevant biographies of Muhammad. How do Christians make the life of Jesus and the first apostles relevant to their own situation?

## The Quran on the Prophet

The following verses in the Quran speak about the character and role of the Prophet Muhammad.

> 62:1–2, *Whatever is in the heavens and on earth, doth declare the Praises and Glory of Allah—the Sovereign, the Holy One, the Exalted in Might, the Wise. It is He Who has sent amongst the Unlettered a messenger from among themselves, to rehearse to them His Signs, to purify them, and to instruct them in Book and Wisdom—although they had been, before, in manifest error;*

> 47:2, *But those who believe and work deeds of righteousness, and believe in the (Revelation) sent down to Muhammad—for it is the Truth from their Lord—He will remove from them their ills and improve their condition.*

> 81:19–21, *Verily this is the word of a most honorable Messenger, Endued with Power, held in honor by the Lord of the Throne, With authority there, (and) faithful to his trust.*

> 4:64–65, *We sent not a messenger, but to be obeyed, in accordance with the leave of Allah. If they had only, when they were unjust to themselves, come unto thee and asked Allah's forgiveness, and the Messenger had asked forgiveness for them, they would have found Allah indeed Oft-returning, Most Merciful. But no, by thy Lord, they can have no (real) Faith, until they make thee judge in all disputes*

*between them, and find in their souls no resistance against thy deci-
sions, but accept them with the fullest conviction.*

53:1-28, *By the Star when it goes down—Your Companion is neither astray nor being misled. Nor does he say (aught) of (his own)
Desire. It is no less than Inspiration sent down to him: he was taught
by one Mighty in Power, endued with Wisdom: for he appeared (in
stately form); while he was in the highest part of the horizon: then he
approached and came closer, and was at a distance of but two bow-
lengths or (even) nearer; so did (Allah) convey the inspiration to His
Servant—(conveyed) what He (meant) to convey. The (Prophet's)
(mind and) heart in no way falsified that which he saw. Will ye then
dispute with him concerning what he saw? For indeed he saw him at
a second descent,near the Lote-tree of the uttermost boundary: near
it is the Garden of Abode. Behold, the Lote-tree was shrouded with
what shrouds. (His) sight never swerved, nor did it go wrong! For
truly did he see, of the Signs of his Lord, the Greatest!*

3:144, *Muhammad is no more than a messenger: many were the
messengers that passed away before him. Is it that if he died or were
slain, will ye then turn back on your heels? If any did turn back on his
heels, not the least harm will he do to Allah. But Allah (on the other
hand) will swiftly reward those who (serve Him) with gratitude.*

7:188, *Say: "I have no power over any good or harm to myself except
as Allah willeth. If I had knowledge of the unseen, I should have
multiplied all good, and no evil should have touched me: I am but a
warner, and a bringer of glad tidings to those who have faith."*

33:40 *Muhammad is not the father of any of your men, but (he is)
the Messenger of Allah, and the Seal of the Prophets: and Allah has
full knowledge of all things.*

## The Quran on Jesus

By comparison Christians may find it interesting to read some of what the
Quran says about Jesus.

3:55–59, *Behold! Allah said: "O Jesus! I will take thee and raise thee
to Myself and clear thee (of the falsehoods) of those who blaspheme;
I will make those who follow thee superior to those who reject faith,
to the Day of Resurrection: Then shall ye all return unto Me, and I
will judge between you of the matters wherein ye dispute. As to those
who reject faith, I will punish them with severe agony in this world*

*and in the Hereafter, nor will they have anyone to help." As to those who believe and work righteousness, Allah will pay them (in full) their reward; but Allah loveth not those who do wrong. This is what we rehearse unto thee of the Signs and the Message of Wisdom." The similitude of Jesus before Allah is as that of Adam; He created him from dust, then said to him: "Be." And he was.*

*4:157, That they said (in boast), "We killed Christ Jesus the son of Mary, the Messenger of Allah." But they killed him not, nor crucified him, but so it was made to appear to them, and those who differ therein are full of doubts, with no (certain) knowledge, but only conjecture to follow, for of a surety they killed him not: nay, Allah raised him up unto Himself; and Allah is Exalted in Power, Wise; and there is none of the People of the Book but must believe in him before his death; and on the Day of Judgment he will be a witness against them . . .*

*4:171, O People of the Book! Commit no excesses in your religion: Nor say of Allah aught but the truth. Christ Jesus the son of Mary was (no more than) a messenger of Allah, and His Word, which He bestowed on Mary, and a Spirit proceeding from Him: so believe in Allah and His messengers. Say not "Three (Trinity)": desist: it will be better for you: for Allah is One God. Glory be to Him: (far exalted is He) above having a son. To Him belong all things in the heavens and on earth. And enough is Allah as a Disposer of affairs.*

*19:16–36, Relate in the Book (the story of) Mary, when she withdrew from her family to a place in the East. She placed a screen (to screen herself) from them; then We sent her Our angel, and he appeared before her as a man in all respects. She said: "I seek refuge from thee to (Allah) Most Gracious: (come not near) if thou dost fear Allah." He said: "Nay, I am only a messenger from thy Lord, (to announce) to thee the gift of a pure son." She said: "How shall I have a son, seeing that no man has touched me, and I am not unchaste?" He said: "So (it will be): thy Lord saith, 'That is easy for Me: and (We wish) to appoint him as a Sign unto men and a Mercy from Us.' It is a matter (so) decreed." So she conceived him, and she retired with him to a remote place. And the pains of childbirth drove her to the trunk of a palm-tree. She cried (in her anguish): "Ah! would that I had died before this! Would that I had been a thing forgotten!" But (a voice) cried to her from beneath the (palm-tree): "Grieve not! for thy Lord hath provided a rivulet beneath thee; "And shake towards thyself the trunk of the palm-tree: It will let fall fresh ripe dates upon thee. So eat and drink and cool (thine) eye. And if thou dost see any man, say, 'I have vowed a fast to (Allah) Most Gracious, and this day will I enter into no talk with any human being'" At length she brought the (babe) to her people, carrying him (in her arms). They said: "O Mary! truly a strange thing has thou brought! O sister of Aaron! Thy father was not a man of evil, nor thy mother a woman unchaste!" But she pointed to the babe. They said: "How can we talk to one who is a child in the cradle?" He said: "I am indeed a servant of Allah. He hath given me revelation and made me a prophet; "And He hath made me blessed wheresoever I be, and hath enjoined on me Prayer and Charity as long as I live; (He hath made me) kind to my mother, and not overbearing or unblest; So peace is on me the day I was born, the day that I die, and the day that I shall be raised up to life (again)!" Such (was) Jesus the son of Mary: (it is) a statement of truth, about which they (vainly) dispute. It is not befitting to (the majesty of) Allah that He should beget a son. Glory be to Him! when He determines a matter, He only says to it, "Be," and it is. Verily Allah is my Lord and your Lord: Him therefore serve ye: this is a Way that is straight.*

*2:253 Those messengers We endowed with gifts, some above others: To one of them Allah spoke; others He raised to degrees (of honor); to Jesus the son of Mary We gave clear (Signs), and strengthened him with the Holy Spirit.*

## Additional Questions

- How does the Quranic view of Jesus agree and disagree with that of the Bible?

- How important is it to Christians that Jesus actually died on the cross, and was not simply taken into heaven as the Quran suggests?

The poems below show both devotion to the Prophet Muhammad and use that devotion to encourage piety. As you read them consider how they resemble, and differ from, the Christian poetry with which you are familiar.

## Tala`a al-Badru `Alayna

The poem below is only one of hundreds of examples of devotion to Muhammad poured out in poetic form. It was written originally in Arabic, and is found with the English translation at http: //www.geocities.com/ahlulbayt14/badr.html.

O Prophet, Peace be upon you.
O Messenger, Peace be upon you.
O Beloved, Peace be upon you.
The Blessings of Allah be upon you.

The full moon has risen over us
From the mountains of al-Wada'.
We shall ever give thanks for it
As long as there will be callers to Allah.

You are a sun, you are a full moon,
You are light upon light,
You are the quintessence of existence,
You are the lamp in every breast

The full moon has risen over us
Eclipsing all other moons.
Such as your beauty we have never seen
No, never, O face of delight!

O My beloved, O Muhammad,
O bridegroom of the East and the West,
The one Allah vindicated and exalted,
O Imam of the Two Directions!

O Prophet, Peace be upon you.
O Messenger, Peace be upon you.
O Beloved, Peace be upon you.
The Blessings of Allah be upon you.

## A Second Poem

This modern poem has much in common with popular Christian doggerel.
It was written in English, apparently by an American Muslim. The source is
http://www.geocities.com/ahlulbayt14/poems.html.

*If Prophet Muhammad (s) visited you*

If Prophet Muhammad (s) visited you
Just for a day or two,
If he came unexpectedly,
I wonder what you'd do,

Oh, I know you'd give your nicest room
To such an honored guest
And all the food you'd serve him,
Would be the very best,

. . . .

But . . . when you saw him coming,
Would you meet him at the door,
With arms outstretched in welcome
To your visitor?

Or . . . would you have to change your clothes
Before you let him in?
Or hide some magazines and put
The Quran where they had been?

Would you still watch the same movies
On your T.V. set?
Or would you switch it off
Before he gets upset?

. . . .

Would you go right on saying the things
You always say?
Would life for you continue,
As it does from day to day?

Would your family squabbles
Keep up their usual pace,
And Would you find it hard each meal
To say a table grace?

Would you keep up each and every prayer
Without putting on a frown?
And would you always jump up early
For prayer at dawn?

. . . .

Would you be glad to have him meet
Your very closest friends?
Or, would you hope they stay away
Until his visit ends?

Would you be glad to have him stay
Forever, on and on?

Or would you sigh with great relief
When he at last was gone?

It might be interesting to know
The things that you would do,
If Prophet Muhammad, in person, came
To spend some time with you

## Additional Questions

- Does the devotion shown to Muhammad have a parallel in Christian literature?
- What is the difference in the attitude Muhammad expressed in the two poems?
- Each poem represents a kind of Muslim spirituality. With which can you most easily identify?

# Chapter 4: The Quran

For Muslims the Quran is not merely a book, but the ongoing event of God's presence with humankind. It is called the "final revelation" and yet it is not merely the last of a series. It is also the sum of God's revelation, complete and sufficient for all time and all humanity. It exists not just on the pages of a book, but eternally with God in heaven, written into the structure of the natural world, and inscribed on the human heart and soul. I attended a display of copies of the Quran in Kuala Lumpur, Malaysia. Part of the display was a tree trunk, which when cut in half displayed patterns that Muslims read as the opening lines of the Quran. Questioning a group of schoolgirls attending the display, I was told that this was less miraculous than representative. One expects to find God's revelation written into creation.

It would not be far wrong to say that while Muhammad's life inspires Muslims to obedience, it is the Quran, experienced constantly in prayer and in the course of daily life, which empowers them. An extract from a meditation by Hasan Askari, related by Neil Robinson in his book *Discovering the Quran,* illustrates this well.[1] Askari was moved to write it when a young friend of his told him about his mother. The mother had never been taught how to read, yet before dawn she would rise and kindle a lamp, unfurl her prayer mat and remove her Quran from its green silk wrapping.

> *"For a long time she would allow her eyes to rest on the two open pages before her. The letters in green ink from right to left, row beneath row, each shape mysteriously captivating, each dot above or below a letter an epitome of the entire scripture, each assembly of letters a group of dervishes raising their hands in zikr, each gap between two enigmatic shapes a leap from this world into the next, and each ending the advent of the day of Resurrection.*
>
> *"She would thus see a thousand images in the procession of that script and would move from vision to vision.*

1. Robinson, *Discovering the Quran,* 24.

*"After spending much time in just looking at the open book, she would then, with strange light glowing on her face, lift her right hand and with the right finger start touching the letters of each line, then another line, to the end of the page. What transpired between the book and that touch, and what knowledge passed, without any mediation of conscious thought, directly into her soul, only the Quran and the strange reciter could know. The entire world stood still at this amazing recital without words, without meaning, without knowledge. With that touch a unity was established between her and the Quran. At that moment she had passed into a state of total identity with the word of God. Her inability to read the scripture was her ability to hear once again: Read! Read, in the name of thy Lord."*

## 1. The Major Themes of the Quran

What captivated the first hearers of the Quran, and still captivates Muslims today, is its ability to lift the problems and possibilities of everyday life into the transcendent realm of God's judgment, mercy, and glory. That message centers on several major themes:

- The necessity that humans acknowledge and praise God,
- The unity of God's revelation in time and space,
- The finality of God's revelation to Muhammad,
- The demand that humans submit to that revelation,
- Muhammad's role as the leader of God's people,
- Islam as belief and practice,
- Islam as a community of God's law, and
- God's final judgment on all humanity, predestination, and the last things.

These themes weave in and out of God's exhortations to humanity, directions on specific issues of the early community, stories of creation, history, legend, and myth. Each of these themes spoke powerfully to the first Muslim community, yet the verses of the Quran came to that community in a fashion that is alien to modern literature. They came neither in the form of rationally presented arguments, nor as powerful narratives. Rather, as Kenneth Cragg points out in his *The Event of the Quran*, they broke into the lives of Muslims at times, and in ways, that transformed their perception of themselves. Perhaps this is the reason that the most popular presentations of the Quran in Muslim societies are in aesthetic forms.

## 2. The Aesthetic Power of the Quran

With its strict ban on iconography, Islam quickly established calligraphy as the chief among its arts. In a thousand different ways the sweeping lines of Arabic script could be shaped into an aesthetic experience, one which was equally forceful for those who were literate and those who were not. In any case, the great majority of Muslims would learn to recognize the "*bismiAllah*" or opening lines of the Quran, the name of the Prophet, or the common phrase, "Praise be upon him" which inevitably followed his name.

The ninety-nine names of God have been shaped into both symbolic and abstract forms that hang in virtually every Muslim household. Verses are woven into honored pieces of clothing, prayer rugs, and tapestries. They form the intricate pattern of tiles on the roof of great mosques and run with supernatural grace around prayer halls. And they have been shaped into charms and amulets believed to protect their bearers from danger and heal their diseases. These verses, dancing before the eye, enchant those who look on them and draw them to contemplate their transcendent source.

Many Muslims have a similar experience when they hear the Quran read, particularly by a talented reader. The aesthetic experience of the written Quran as a doorway to the divine is matched by the aesthetic experience of the Quran sung or chanted. The sound of the chanted Quran is the first thing a Muslim child hears, and that sound in the constantly repeated phrases of daily prayer penetrates and forms her or his soul long before the meaning of the words will begin to form the mind.[2]

Chanting the Quran is an art in itself, and one that virtually every Muslim learns in at least rudimentary form. Strict rules (which have little to do with preserving the literal meaning) guide inflection and breathing. Differing schools preserve closely the variations in the pronunciation of classical Arabic.

> *Muhammad is the messenger of Allah, and those who are with him are strong against Unbelievers, (but) compassionate amongst each other. Thou wilt see them bow and prostrate themselves (in prayer), seeking Grace from Allah and (His) Good Pleasure. Quran 48:29*

2. Nasr, ed., *Islamic Spirituality*, 4.

In the Islamic world there are hundreds of Quran-reading competitions, crowned by an annual international competition. These as well as public recitations and readings on the TV and radio lift up to the public the most talented chanters. These "stars" are widely available on cassette tape, and now CD, and their readings can be purchased in virtually any Muslim bookstore. As with the calligraphic presentation of the Quran, the intellectual process of reading, understanding, and interpreting is overtaken by the direct experience of God's numinous power breaking in on human life.[3] This experience mirrors Muhammad's original experience of the Quran, when God's revelation was experienced not merely as words, but as a soul- and body-shattering power like the ringing of a huge bell within the skull, or an overpowering pressure on the heart.

> *Whoever submits his whole self to Allah, and is a doer of good, has grasped indeed the firmest hand-hold: and with Allah shall all things return. Quran 31:22*

This emphasis on the power of the Quran through not only its intellectual meaning, but also its powerful aesthetic, makes it difficult for many Christians to appreciate. As Karen Armstrong points out in her *History of God*, Muslims have never gone through a period such as the Western Enlightenment, where the value of language has been reduced to a role in rational discourse. For Muslims spiritual and religious truth is communicated to the soul through the Quran at many levels.

This helps explain why for Muslims the Quran exists as such only in Arabic. Only Arabic can preserve the full impact of the revelation on Muhammad, and its status as an eternal revelation that existed before all time with God. One title for the Quran is "The Mother of All Books" and for Muslims it is the primal language of the human soul, the first and the sum of all significant human speech. Theologically the Quran revealed to Muhammad (in Arabic) is something like the *Logos* incarnate in Jesus Christ. It is, as the gospel accounts of the life of Jesus are for Christians, the irreducible minimum for an understanding of God's self-revelation. And it is the fullness of what God is for the world.

For this reason until recently there was never a strong drive to translate the Quran within the Muslim world. Instead Muslims from the non-Arabic world have been encouraged to learn Arabic at least to the extent necessary to sound out its words. This also means that when the Quran

3. Ibid., 5.

has been translated it is primarily by individuals with widely varying competency in both the Quran and the receptor language. No translation of the Quran into English has the scholarly, linguistic, and ecclesial clout of the best English translations of the Bible. As a result, interpretations of the Quran into English and other languages convey little of the power that the original has for Muslims.

## 3. The Science of Quran Interpretation

Christians may find it easier to appreciate the intense intellectual challenge, and satisfaction, of the process of interpreting the meaning of the Quran, which is the most fundamental Islamic science.

> *And what will explain to thee what the Day of Judgment is? Again, what will explain to thee what the Day of Judgment is? (It will be) the Day when no soul shall have power (to do) aught for another: For the Command, that Day, will be (wholly) with Allah. Quran 82:17–19*

It is a science that is, however, somewhat different from the study of biblical interpretation. Muhammad's revelations were shared with, and memorized by, his closest followers as they occurred. Muslims maintain that by the time of his death an agreed body of revelation called the Quran existed, and shortly afterwards was written down. The very few variations that existed (amounting to a handful of verses) were resolved within decades of his death, and since that time there has been a single, universally known, text to the Quran. Thus, unlike the Bible, no Muslim science of "textual criticism," which discerns the earliest or best-preserved text, is considered necessary. And unlike the Bible, the historical and cultural context of each revelation is well known. The occasion for each revelation was remembered by the earliest Muslims and passed on in a separate tradition. In many cases these traditions included Muhammad's own interpretation of the verses, which were naturally taken as authoritative.[4]

Still, interpreting the Quran requires several types of knowledge, including the context of the verse in the history of the early Muslim community and an in-depth knowledge of the *hadith*.[5] Central to interpretation

---

4. In recent years some Western scholars have attempted to apply the types of critical techniques long employed in evaluating the history of the Bible to the Quran. Their findings do not always accord with what Muslims accept about its provenance.

5. Knowing and evaluating the *hadith* is a science in itself, with its own particular

is a mastery of the rich meaning of its words and the complex grammar of poetic Arabic. This knowledge is preserved in early Muslim guides to interpretation and commentaries, which were continually rewritten and explained, so that a true scholar of the Quran must be familiar with these as well. And finally, the tradition of interpretation, found in a wealth of commentaries from the first three centuries of Islam, must be taken into account in any modern interpretation. These explain the relation of apparently contradictory verses in the Quran as well as the rules that allow particular verses to be applied in particular situations.

> Verily We have sent thee in truth, as a bearer of glad tidings, and as a warner: and there never was a people, without a warner having lived among them (in the past). Quran 35:24

The result is a rich science of interpretation that becomes for many Muslims a witness to the majesty and finality of God's revelation. Once mastered this science can become a world in itself; an ideal world in which the whole of God's plan for humankind is unfolded. It is not an entirely consistent world, but then this is also seen as a witness to the way in which God's word is shaped to many different human situations. For many Muslims this world of interpretation is seductive. It draws them into an idealized world sanctioned by God and reflecting both the simplicity of God's unity and the complexity of God's will for humanity. Those who enter into this world easily believe that they have entered into a numinous and transcendent realm created by a super-rationality beyond the sciences created by mere human knowledge and observation.

## 4. The Quran and Science

At the same time it is important for modern Muslims that the Quran, when interpreted, be consistent with and even a precursor to the findings of modern science. In the nineteenth century, when the technological and economic power of the colonizing countries overwhelmed most Muslim lands, there were Muslims tempted to retreat into spirituality. Leaders like Jamal al Din al Afghani resisted this, rallying young Muslims to their religion by claiming that it was not only the final revelation, but that it

---

rules and multiple overlapping collections of sayings. http://www.muttaqun.com/scienceofhadith.html has a brief introduction to this science. (Winter Park, Florida, Muttaqun Foundation, no date.)

was the revelation of rationality and empirical science. He reminded them how Greek philosophy and logic, and the sciences of medicine, astronomy, mathematics, and navigation were preserved and advanced by Muslim scholars when Christendom was sunk in the superstitions of the Dark Ages. Much of the foundation of modern Western science was built on the work of Muslims.

> *This day have I perfected your religion for you, completed My favor upon you, and have chosen for you Islam as your religion. Quran 5:3*

Since his time the claim that Islam has no quarrel with science has become a common apologetic stance of Muslims, and justification of their faith. Muslims criticize Christian biblical interpretation that either denies the literal meaning of the text or accepts it in defiance of a rational and scientific understanding of the world. The Quran, it is maintained, has no such conflicts.

It must be noted, however, that this criticism is somewhat ingenuous. With either the Quran or the Bible the key issue is how to fit a literalist interpretation with a scientific and rational understanding of God and the world. The anthropomorphic attributes of God found in the Quran (God speaks, has hands and feet, feels, etc.) have always conflicted with assertions in the Quran that God is beyond all human characteristics, as well as with more rational understandings of God that preclude the possession of human attributes.

> *To thee We sent the Scripture in truth, confirming the scripture that came before it, and guarding it in safety: so judge between them by what Allah hath revealed, and follow not their vain desires, diverging from the Truth that hath come to thee. To each among you have we prescribed a Law and an Open Way . . . Quran 5:48*

This conflict was the subject of great controversy in the first three centuries of Islam and was resolved when the classical schools of interpretation required Muslims to simply believe in the contradictory assertions that God is wholly other than anything in the created world, and that nonetheless every word about God in the Quran is literally true.

Commentators who sought non-literal, but philosophically consistent interpretations (such as the Mu'tazilites), were ultimately condemned as heretics. It is true that the particular conflict between the natural sciences and revealed knowledge that has bedeviled Christian attitudes toward modernity is not found in the same form in Islam. Yet the underlying problem of maintaining the authority of a text when rational reflection and human experience undermines its claim to literal truth is similar in both religions.

Intellectuals like Fazlur Rahman have been interested in pushing beyond an apologetic assertion that the Quran is consistent with modern science to the deeper problem of whether revelation has a role to play in a science-based civilization. He and others have suggested that there needs to be a thoroughgoing "Islamization of knowledge" that would overcome the weaknesses of a dehumanizing and materialistic scientific understanding of the world. In his book *Islam and Modernity,* Rahman suggests rebuilding the structure of human knowledge so that revelation has a central role, faith is regarded as a legitimate means of knowing, and metaphysics interact fruitfully with the physical sciences in describing the nature of reality.

Such a project overthrows the intellectual developments of the last 200 years in the West, and is radical in its reach. It also has appeal for Muslims as it suggests that a renewed Islamic civilization is self-sufficient, self-legitimizing, and restores the Islamic intellectual tradition to its rightful place. Already a number of Islamic institutions and universities have been built wholly or partially on this basis, with Islamic sociology, Islamic economics, Islamic law, and other "Islamic" sciences competing (or cooperating) with their non-Islamic counterparts. These projects vary in their approaches to implementing Rahman's ambitious agenda, while holding in common the ideal that the Quran is not only consistent with human reason but is the font of all knowledge of reality.

## 5. Esoteric Interpretation

Some Muslims have not been content with building their spirituality on the literal and rational interpretations of the Quran. For Shī'ite Muslims and Sufis the Quran itself bears witness to an almost infinite range of esoteric meanings and influences on the soul questing for God. The most suggestive clue to the importance of esoteric interpretation comes in those *surah* (chapters) of the Quran that contain a series of apparently random letters at the beginning. These letters form no known word and have no obvious acrostic meaning, yet they are clearly part of God's revelation. This suggests to Muslims that men and women with particular spiritual discernment can grasp meanings in the Quran deeper than those discovered by a literal reading.

The unfolding of these meanings, a process called *ta'wil*, begins by finding the symbolic meanings of individual letters, words, and numbers. The intention of such interpretation is not so much to provide an alternative to form of commentary as it is to penetrate the reader's being with the Divine presence, of which the Quran as a whole is the most important symbol.[6] One level of symbolism in the Quran is made up of objects symbolizing God's presence and creative activity, such as the sky, sun, moon, and stars. Through these an elaborate system of correspondences can be established so that virtually every earthly reality reveals something about a spiritual, or heavenly, counterpart. Ordinary objects are also taken to have a symbolic significance in the Quran, in particular the "pen" and the "tablet" that relate not only to mundane objects, but to the whole process of language, writing, and revelation.

> *If Allah had so willed, He would have made you a single people, but (His plan is) to test you in what He hath given you: so strive as in a race in all virtues. The goal of you all is to Allah; it is He that will show you the truth of the matters in which ye dispute . . . Quran 5:48*

At another level individual letters are believed to have a special meaning. Because all the letters in Arabic have a numerical value, an elaborate science of numerology has arisen to discover hidden meanings in the arrangements of letters in particular *surah*, the number of letters, words, and sentences in various *surah* and the Quran as a whole, and of course the combinations of all of these.

Christians of a rationalist bent may well find this kind of search for meaning in a text excessively imaginative and even arbitrary. For many Muslims, however, spiritual discernment and imagination are simply two sides of the same coin. Esoteric commentaries have stood the test of time not because they stood up to rational scrutiny, but because their writers were men and women of known charisma. And they have over the centuries continued to open the way for a deeper experience of God's presence to those who read and meditated on them.

For Shī'ite Muslims there is another reason for their effectiveness. Shī'ites believe that God endowed the descendants of the Prophet Muhammad with a special spiritual discernment that allowed for revealed truth to flow through them. When the last of these leaders, or Imams, passed into a hidden state of existence, his gift became available to his followers through

---

6. Nasr, ed., *Islamic Spirituality,* 26.

their greatest religious leaders, called *ayatollah*. These men are gifted in esoteric interpretation by their communication with the hidden Imam and become conduits for truths beneath and beyond the literal text of the Quran and words of Muhammad. [7]

## 6. Conclusion

Just as Muhammad is no mere prophet, but the perfect concretization of the Prophetic Substance, so the Quran is no mere written record of prophecy for Muslims. Even less is it just an account of Muhammad's faith. Rather it is the "crystallization" of everything God is for God's creation: the substance of true religion. It is the wellspring of personal faith and religious devotion, human civilization and social order, and every form of spirituality. One might well say that Islam, submission to Allah, is the submission of the soul that lets itself be charmed, enchanted, and possessed by the Quran, just as Muhammad did when the angel Gabriel delivered the first revelation to him in the cave at Hirah. Those of us who have not felt that spell, and do not know that enchantment, can imagine only a little of a Muslim's faith. And in our relationships with Muslims we must tread as carefully in our attitudes and comments toward the Quran as we would in our criticisms of one beloved to their lover.

## Guide for Further Study

Review the key themes of the chapter. If members of the study group have questions about the these key themes it would be good to discuss these first.

---

7. None of these ideas are unknown in Christianity, although they take a somewhat different form. A recent best seller, Drosnin's *The Bible Code*, gained its popularity because so many modern Christians are willing to believe that hidden within the Bible is a numerical and symbolic code that reveals meanings far beyond the literal. Nor is it illogical that the meanings of God's word cannot be exhausted by a literal, and limited, interpretation. In the history of the church there have also been movements that sought an inspired meaning to Scripture revealed to those who were guided by the Holy Spirit to a deeper meaning. Christ's promise to send an advocate, or counselor, to reveal the meaning of his words has always suggested to some Christians that Scripture could not be exhausted by rational commentary, and that spiritual discernment might be as important as mastery of the literal text in finding its meaning.

## Key Themes

- The Quran, experienced as a miracle of eloquence and beauty, inspires and empowers Muslims to be obedient to God.

- The major themes of the Quran focus on: 1. the necessity that humans and acknowledge and praise God, 2. the unity of God's revelation in time and space, 3. the finality of God's revelation to Muhammad, 4. the demand that humans submit to that revelation, 5. Muhammad's role as the leader of God's people, 6. Islam as belief and practice, 7. Islam as a community of God's law, 8. God's final judgment on all humanity, and the predestination of every person to paradise or hell.

- Interpretation of the Quran is considered a rational science in Islam and is based on an understanding of the Arab language in Muhammad's time, the collecting and evaluating of prophetic traditions, and a mastery of the tradition of interpretation of the Quran.

- Muslims consider the teaching of the Quran, taken literally, as consistent with modern science and scientific method.

- Some Muslims also interpret the Quran symbolically and allegorically in order to draw hidden meanings from it that can lead them to a mystical knowledge of God and God's world.


## Final Questions for Discussion

- How does a Christian reading of the Bible differ from the Muslim reading of the Quran mentioned in the introduction to this chapter?

- Which major themes of the Quran do Christians find in the Bible? Which are different?

- How is the Christian understanding of the origin of the Bible different from that of Muslim understandings of the origin of the Quran? How is it the same?

- What do Christians expect to gain from reading the Bible? How does that differ from what Muslims gain by reading the Quran? How is it the same?

- What are some ways that Christians have used the Bible in art? What could we learn from Muslims about the relationship between God's word and aesthetics?

- An esoteric interpretation of the Quran expresses in part a confidence that God's revelation should have a plenitude of meaning. How does this compare with Christian attitudes about the Bible?

## Additional Readings

The readings below come from two Muslim reformers who are concerned that the Quran be the basis of Islamic society, yet who recognize that traditional interpretations of the Quran have obscured what they regard as its fundamental message. The interview with Shaheen gives us a view of the Quran from a committed laywoman who in a different way looks forward to the realization of the Quranic ideal.

Rahman, Fazlur. *Islam and Modernity*. Chicago: University of Chicago Press, 1982.

### Excerpts from Chapter 4

1. Metaphysics, in my understanding, is the unity of knowledge and the meaning and orientation this unity gives to life. If this unity is the unity of knowledge, how can it be all that subjective? It is a faith grounded in knowledge.

   The Muslims' aim of Islamicizing the several fields of learning cannot be really fulfilled unless Muslims effectively perform the intellectual task of elaborating an Islamic metaphysics on the basis of the Quran. An overall world view of Islam has to be first, if provisionally, attempted if various specific fields of intellectual endeavor are to cohere as informed by Islam. (p. 132)

2. Yet none of this means that any significant interpretation of the Quran can be absolutely monolithic. Nothing could be further from the truth. For one thing, we know from numerous reports that the Prophet's Companions themselves sometimes understood certain Quranic verses differently, and this was within his knowledge. Further, the Quran, as I have often reiterated, is a document that grew within a background, from the flesh and blood of actual history; it is therefore both as "straightforward" and as organically coherent as life. (p. 144)

3. The Quran calls itself "guidance for mankind" (*hudan li'lnas*) and by the same term designates earlier revealed documents. Its central moral concept for man in *taqwa*, which is usually translated as "piety" or "Godfearingness" but which in the various Quranic contexts may be defined as "a mental state of responsibility from which an agent's actions proceed but which recognizes that the criterion of judgment upon them lies outside him." The whole business of the Quran appears to be centered on the attempt to induce such a state in man. The idea of a secular law, insofar as it makes this state indifferent to its obedience, which is consequently conceived in mechanical terms, is the very abnegation of *taqwa*. The increasingly chaotic state of affairs in Western societies and the gradual erosion of an inner sense of responsibility represent a complex situation, but this situation is undoubtedly linked with a process through which law ceased to maintain any organic relation to morality. (p. 155)

## Additional Questions

• For Rahman finding the "world view" of the Quran is essential to developing modern Muslim knowledge. Is the worldview of the Bible equally essential to Christian knowledge of the world? Can the biblical message fit with many different "worldviews"?

• Do you agree with Rahman that secular law must be related to morality, and morality with revelation?

## Wadud-Muhsin, Amina. *Quran and Woman.*
Shah Alam, Malaysia: Penerbit Fajar Bakti, 1992.

### Excerpts from the Introduction

1. No method of Quranic exegesis is fully objective. Each exegete makes some subjective choices. Some details of their interpretations reflect their subjective choices and not necessarily the intent of the text. Yet, often, no distinction is made between text and interpretation. I put interpretations of woman in the Quran into three categories: 'traditional', reactive, and holistic.

    The first category of Quranic interpretation I call 'traditional.' . . .They begin with the first verse of the first chapter and proceed to the second verse of the first chapter one verse at a time until the end of the Book. Little or no effort is made to recognize themes and to discuss the relationship of the Quran to itself, thematically.

However, what concerns me most about 'traditional' *tafsir* is that they were exclusively written by males. This means that men and men's experiences were included and women and women's experiences were either excluded or interpreted through the male vision perspective, desire, or needs of woman. . . .

The second category of Quranic interpretation concerned with the issue of woman consists primarily of modern scholars' reactions to severe handicaps for woman as an individual and as a member of society which have been attributed to the text. In this category are many women and/or persons opposed to the Quranic message (or more precisely, to Islam) altogether . . .

The interpretations which reconsider the whole method of Quranic exegesis with regard to various modern social, moral, economic and political concerns including the issue of woman make up the final category. . . . This category is relatively new, and there has been no substantial consideration of the particular issue of woman in the light of the entire Quran and its major principles. (pp. 1–3)

2. A hermeneutical model is concerned with three aspects of the text, in order to support its conclusions: 1. the context in which the text was written (in the case of the Quran, in which it was revealed); 2. the grammatical composition of the text (how it says what it says) and 3. the whole text, its Weltanschauung or worldview . . .

However, in order for the Quran to achieve its objective to act as a catalyst affecting behaviour in society, each social context must understand the fundamental and unchangeable principles of that text, and then implement them in their own unique reflection . . .

Therefore, to force it to have a single cultural perspective—even the cultural perspective of the original community of the Prophet—severely limits its application and contradicts the stated universal purpose of the Book itself. (pp. 5, 6)

3. Although there are distinctions between men and women, I argue that they are not of their essential natures. More importantly, I argue against the values that have been attributed to these distinctions. Such attributed values describe women as weak, inferior [and] inherently

evil, intellectually incapable, and spiritually lacking. These evaluations have been used to claim that women are unsuitable for performing certain tasks, or for functioning in some ways in society.

The Quran does not attempt to annihilate the differences between men and women . . . In fact, compatible mutually supportive functional relationships between men and women can be seen as part of the goal of the Quran with regard to society. However, the Quran does not propose or support a singular role or single definition of a set of roles, exclusively for each gender across every culture. (pp. 7–8)

## Additional Questions

- For Wadud it is necessary to find a "worldview" of the Quran that is not the same as the worldview of any particular society, including that of the Prophet. Do you think it is possible to find a revealed worldview different from any held by humans?

- Is there a "biblical worldview" different from that of Jesus and his disciples?

- Wadud says that all interpretation is subjective. Does this mean only women can understand some aspects of the Quran? The Bible?

- What is the difference between men and women in the Bible? Is this different or the same as the difference Wadud finds in the Quran?

## Khan, Nihat Said, ed. *Voices Within*. Lahore, Pakistan: ASR, 1992.

### Excerpts from an interview with Shaheen, pp.89–102.

Shaheen: . . . The Quran basically gives the ultimate goals, where human destiny should be leading to.

Q: But aren't those very similar to other religions? All religions have a basic morality.

Shaheen: But there are certain things which are taken further: for instance, humankind forms one family. That is the ultimate goal, how can we establish a human family? We are today divided into regional, tribal units. And economically, every living being, not only human being, must have his basic needs fulfilled as a matter of right, not on the basis of charity, or sympathy.

Q: But the Quran also says that there can be slaves.

Shaheen: The Quran says things have to be done gradually. . . . The Quran says you must reach there slowly through education, by certain laws, by gradual changes in the existing law. The Quran has given certain guidelines for that transitory period. For instance, don't give slaves emancipation suddenly; you have to do it gradually, adjust them to the situation of freedom first. . . .

Shaheen: As regards women the Quran does emphasize that the maintenance of the family, as a matter of duty, is the responsibility of the man. There is no equivalent duty on women. You can earn, do what you like, but no one can force you to go out to work and support the children.

Q: Isn't this inequality?

Shaheen: We're imagining things as they are today. The ideal thing that will come about is so different, so difficult to visualize, but when one arrives at that situation no one will be economically dominant to anyone else.

Q: But within Islam, as a woman, does it give you a reason for existence, an explanation of life, an idealism? What is your own personal thing and what does God do for you?

Shaheen: For me the permanent values are the vision towards which I must go. I think they're so beautiful, in the sense that I must do everything to fight, in the present context, apartheid, poverty. I can see a dictator in my country, or any other country, then I must go beyond my country. It has to be a universal movement. So I'm moving in that direction. That vision beckons me. And, I think, there has to be a vision, whatever that vision may be. (pp. 97–100)

## Additional Questions

- In the interview the questioner points out that the Quran as a source of ideals is in tension with certain specific aspects of its teaching, particularly with regard to women. Is there a similar problem for Christians with the Bible? How does Shaheen explain this tension? How would you?

## The Quran on the Quran

10:36, *This Quran is not such as can be produced by other than Allah. On the contrary it is a confirmation of (revelations) that went before it, and a fuller explanation of the Book—wherein there is no doubt—from the Lord of the Worlds.*

12:1-3, *Alif. Lám. Rá. These are the Verses of the Perspicuous Book. We have sent it down as an Arabic Quran, in order that ye may learn wisdom. We do relate unto thee the most beautiful of stories, in that We reveal to thee this (portion of the) Quran: before this, thou too was among those who knew it not.*

17:45-46, *When thou dost recite the Quran, We put, between thee and those who believe not in the Hereafter, a veil invisible: And We put coverings over their hearts (and minds) lest they should understand the Quran, and deafness into their ears: when thou dost mention thy Lord and Him alone in the Quran, they turn on their backs, fleeing (from the Truth).*

17:81–82, *And say: "Truth has (now) arrived, and Falsehood perished: for Falsehood is (by its nature) bound to perish." We send down (stage by stage) in the Quran that which is a healing and a mercy to those who believe: to the unjust it causes nothing but loss after loss.*

27:1–2, *These are verses of the Quran,-a book that makes (things) clear; a Guide: and Glad Tidings for the believers . . .*

69:40–46, *That this is verily the word of an honored messenger; it is not the word of a poet: little it is ye believe! Nor is it the word of a soothsayer: little admonition it is ye receive. (This is) a Message sent down from the Lord of the Worlds. And if the messenger were to invent any sayings in Our name, We should certainly seize him by his right hand, and We should certainly then cut off the artery of his heart.*

44:1–8, *Há Mím. By the Book that makes things clear—We sent it down during a blessed night: for We (ever) wish to warn (against Evil). In that (night) is made distinct every affair of wisdom, by command, from Us. For We (ever) send (revelations), as Mercy from thy Lord: for He hears and knows (all things); the Lord of the heavens and the earth and all between them, if ye (but) have an assured faith. There is no god but He: It is He Who gives life and gives death, The Lord and Cherisher to you and your earliest ancestors . . .*

*85:21–22 Nay, this is a Glorious Quran, (Inscribed) in a Tablet Preserved!*

## Additional Questions

- The Quran speaks about itself dozens of times. In the New Testament there are relatively few references to written Scripture or revelation because the focus is on Jesus Christ as God's Word. Read 2 Timothy 3:16–17, 2 Peter 1:20–21, and John 1:1. How would you describe the difference between a Christian understanding of revelation and that of Islam?

## Quran on Women

*4:1, O mankind! fear your Guardian Lord, Who created you from a single person, created out of it his mate, and from them twain scattered (like seeds) countless men and women—fear Allah, through Whom ye demand your mutual (rights), and (be heedful) the wombs (that bore you): for Allah ever watches over you.*

*4:32, And in no wise covet those things in which Allah Hath bestowed His gifts more freely on some of you than on others: to men is allotted what they earn, and to women what they earn: But ask Allah of His bounty. For Allah hath full knowledge of all things.*

*3:195, And their Lord hath accepted of them, and answered them: "Never will I suffer to be lost the work of any of you, be he male or female: Ye are members, one of another: Those who have left their homes, or been driven out therefrom, or suffered harm in My Cause, or fought or been slain—verily, I will blot out from them their iniquities, and admit them into Gardens with rivers flowing beneath—a reward from Allah, and from Allah is the best of rewards."*

*4:124, If any do deeds of righteousness—be they male or female—and have faith, they will enter Heaven, and not the least injustice will be done to them.*

*9:68, Allah hath promised the Hypocrites men and women, and the rejecters of Faith, the fire of Hell: Therein shall they dwell: Sufficient is it for them: for them is the curse of Allah, and an enduring punishment.*

9:71, *The Believers, men and women, are protectors one of another: they enjoin what is just, and forbid what is evil: they observe regular prayers, pay Zakat, and obey Allah and His Messenger. On them will Allah pour His mercy: for Allah is Exalted in power, Wise.*

4:34, *Men are the protectors and maintainers of women, because Allah has given the one more (strength) than the other, and because they support them from their means. Therefore the righteous women are devoutly obedient, and guard in (the husband's) absence what Allah would have them guard. As to those women on whose part ye fear disloyalty and ill-conduct, admonish them (first), (next), refuse to share their beds, (and last) beat them (lightly); but if they return to obedience, seek not against them means (of annoyance): For Allah is Most High, Great (above you all).*

33:59, *O Prophet! Tell thy wives and daughters, and the believing women, that they should cast their outer garments over their persons (when out of doors): that is most convenient, that they should be known (as such) and not molested. And Allah is Oft-Forgiving, Most Merciful.*

24:60 *Such elderly women as are past the prospect of marriage— there is no blame on them if they lay aside their (outer) garments, provided they make not a wanton display of their beauty: but it is best for them to be modest: and Allah is One Who sees and knows all things.*

## Additional Questions

- Reading the Quran verses on women one can see why some Muslim women maintain that the general principle of equality is firm, and should be the basis for judgments of how to manage particular situation. How do Christians understand the relationship between equality before God and equality and equal opportunity in social roles? How do you understand biblical principals to be the same, or different, from those found in the Quran?

Poetry can also express both Muslim reverence for the Quran, and the role it plays in shaping their spirituality.

Hafiz. "Divan-i-Hafiz." In *Teachings of Hafiz,* translated by Gertrude Bell.

Divan-i-Hafiz

From Canaan Joseph shall return, whose face
A little time was hidden: weep no more—
Oh, weep no more! In sorrow's dwelling-place
The roses yet shall spring from the bare floor!
And heart bowed down beneath a secret pain -
Oh stricken heart! Joy shall return again,
Peace to the love-tossed brain—oh, weep no more!

Oh, weep no more! For once again Life's Spring
Shall throne her to the meadows green, and o'er
Her head the minstrel of the night shall fling
A canopy of rose leaves, score on score.
The secret of the world thou shalt not learn,
And yet behind the veil Love's fire may burn—
Weep'st thou? Let hope return and weep no more!

Today may pass, tomorrow pass, before
The turning wheel give me my heart's desire;
Heaven's self shall change, and turn not evermore
The universal wheel of Fate in ire.
Oh Pilgrim nearing Mecca's holy fane,
The thorny maghilan wounds thee in vain,
The desert blooms again—oh, weep no more!

What though the river of mortality
Round the unstable house of Life doth roar,
Weep not, oh heart, Noah shall pilot thee,
And guide thine ark to the desired shore!
The goal lies far, and perilous is thy road,
Yet every path leads to that same abode
Where thou shalt drop thy load—oh, weep no more!

Mine enemies have persecuted me,
My love has turned and fled from out my door—
God counts our tears and knows our misery;
Ah, weep not! He has heard thy weeping sore.
And chained in poverty and plunged in night,
Oh Hafiz, take thy Koran and recite
Litanies infinite, and weep no more!

Additional Questions

- The author finds solace in the chanting of the Quran, and a return to God's verities. Do Christians ever turn to the Bible in the same way?

Kahf, Mohja. "'The Water of Hajar' and Other Poems." In *Muslim World*, edited by Jane I. Smith and Ibrahim Abu Rabi', Vol. 91, 2001.

*The Water of Hajar*

After abandonment
After the blow
that brings the head to the ground
and breaks the teeth,
after the god who requires blood and obedience,
how do you find water?
It has no content

It cools the lips
and moves without words
It is almost not visible
between thorn and rock

Where on this earth
is the water of Hajar,
the water that came
up from the ground,
from the ground of Hajar

given
freely, freely
by the God of Hajar

*Mary's Glade*

*And the pains of childbrith drove her to the trunk of a palm tree
She cried, "Would that I had died before this and been a thing
forgotten and out of sight!" But a voice from beneath called to
her, Grieve not! For your Lord has provided rivulet beneath you
And shake towards yourself the trunk of the palm tree: It will let
fall fresh ripe dates upon you. so eat and drink and cool your eye
(Quran: Maryam 23:6)*

If I could find a glade for my despair

And hide myself like some forgotten thing
By some dead tree trunk equally despised
And hear no more and none to hear from me,
Maryam, would water rush out from the spring?

What fruits would drop for me and what voice bid
Me drink, and eat, and live, Mary? From where
Would comfort come when I have none to give?
If I could find a glade

Like yours, Maryam, where palm trees' fronds are made
To shield young friendless women from cruel eyes
And tenderly to give them holy shade—
But why should I be granted such a place?
And would the palm leaves bend?
Mary, tell me, If I could find a glade

## Additional Questions

- Mohja Kahf is a contemporary poet who weaves Quranic themes into her reflections on womanhood—yet another way in which the Quranic ideal is appropriated by Muslims. How have Christians made use of the Bible as a source of artistic and poetic expression?

# Chapter 5: The Quranic Generation

Muslims have long resisted portraying the men and women who surrounded Muhammad in pictures, and those portrayals that exist make little effort at realism. There is a strong awareness of how easily iconography becomes idolatry. Yet all Muslims are familiar with the character of the men and women of the Quranic generation, as well as their heroic exploits and personal piety. Closer to the struggles of ordinary men and women of faith than Muhammad, their lives provide abiding models of Muslim life, just as their names are those most often given to Muslim children. Together, each with his or her own particular strengths, they personify the variety of personal ideals that Muslims hold. In the individual struggles of the first generation to live according to their confession, Muslims find inspiration to overcome their own challenges.

---

*The Muslim Calendar*

*The Islamic year is based on the lunar cycle, consisting of twelve months of twenty-nine or thirty days each, totaling 353 or 354 days. Each new month begins at the sighting of a new moon. Since this year is shorter than a solar year, Muslim holidays progress by eleven days each solar year. The numbering of Muslim years begins with the Hijrah in 622 CE.*

*2012–2013 was the Muslim year 1434*

---

As a generation, these first followers of Muhammad have a collective significance not unlike that of the apostles for Christians. Their firsthand association with the Prophet is assumed to have endued them with a special portion of his *barakah* or blessedness. For many Muslims they would be regarded as the first saints: men and women whose spiritual influence endured beyond death, and who could bless Muslims from beyond the grave. Controversy surrounds the practice of praying at the tombs of

these and other Muslim saints. Among some of the orthodox such practices are heretical and are strongly condemned. Yet they persist in almost
every Muslim culture.

This Quranic generation is also central to the issue of authority in Islam, and again in this respect is similar to the apostles in early Christianity.
They comprise the generation that received the Quran from Muhammad,
memorized it, and passed it on. When the final version of the Quran was
fixed shortly after Muhammad's death, its purity and correctness were a
product of their ability to recall and agree on what Muhammad had related
to them. They were also the most authoritative source of the Sunnah of the
Prophet, and no tradition about his life is fully accepted if it did not originate with one, and preferably more, of them. So the legal and theological
framework of Islam, while drawing on the Quran and Sunnah as its primary sources, depends secondarily on the reliability of this first generation
of Muslims. The Muslim insistence that modern historiography vindicates
the assertion that these first witnesses to Islam were reliable is often used as
an apologetic point in conflicts between Muslims and Christians, over the
validity of their respective Scriptures and traditions.

Muslims are well aware that this first generation struggled, with less
and less effect, to preserve the purity of Islam. The community had its serious divisions, traitors, and setbacks. Yet when this generation is seen as an
ideal each setback becomes a warning for future Muslims, and each victory over adversity an indication of both God's approval and the emergence
of the true path of faith. Perhaps most importantly, the core members of
Muhammad's followers are depicted as overcoming their personal rivalries
and misunderstandings to stand united for the faith against all its enemies.
They thus became the means by which Islam spread, almost miraculously,
across the Arabian world, and began to overcome the great empires that
surrounded it. The Muslim society they founded could not compare in
grandeur with the Muslim civilization that followed. Yet to future generations of Muslims none would excel the first in spiritual insight, piety, and
obedience to God. In some way they have always been the models for the
*ummah,* the community of God's people.

## 1. The First Followers of the Prophet

The story of the first generation begins even before the death of Muhammad, as each of the most important characters played a role in helping

Muhammad's movement develop. First is Khatijah, his wife, who encouraged him and comforted him when he was overwhelmed with the first revelations of the Quran. His uncle Abu Talib is also an important figure: protecting the Prophet from enemies both inside and outside the clan. All of the other first associates are known by name, including Waraqah, a Christian cousin of Khatijah whose sympathy for Muhammad forms part of the Muslim ideal, and al-Arqam, who opened his house to the first followers of Muhammad. Also important to Muslims who seek precedents for Muslim life in a pluralist environment are the Muslims whom Muhammad sent to Christian Abyssinia to avoid persecution in Mecca. Their courage and exemplary behavior, as well as the treaty establishing their rights as a religious minority, is seen by some as an important precedent for modern Muslims.[1]

The period of persecution in Mecca, which lasted from 615 to 622, proved the character of many in the first generation. It also provided the first idealized enemy of Islam in the form of Abu Jahl, who led the persecution of the Muslims. When he was later killed in battle against the Muslims, along with other leading opponents of Muhammad, the Prophet and later generations saw this as a vindication of their cause.

In 622, at the invitation of leaders from the oasis of Yathrib, Muhammad and his followers moved secretly out of Mecca to Yathrib. Muhammad then took leadership of the various communities living there. Subsequent military conflicts with forces from Mecca would turn many of the first followers into military heroes as well as religious pioneers. In the struggles with Mecca weaknesses of personal and community character would also be revealed, sometimes in ways which later become models of Muslim disappointment and conflict. Certain Muslims maintained their sympathy with the Meccan enemies of Muhammad, and their treachery and hypocrisy became an example of evil. One of the Arab-Jewish tribes in Yathrib was also accused of plotting against Muhammad and was massacred, forming an enduring image of both the Muslim problem with Jews and what some saw as a justified response to treasonous duplicity. It is a legacy many modern Muslims would prefer to leave as history rather than precedent. On other hand, some opponents of Muhammad, notably Abu Sayuf, later had a change of heart and worked actively for peace between the Meccans and Muhammad's followers. Such conversions are yet another part of the ideal of Quranic generation.

1. Ramadan, *To Be a European Muslim*, 124.

Muhammad finally returned to Mecca as its conqueror in 630, after its leading citizens submitted to his military superiority without fighting. From this point on his chief lieutenants began to build renown by leading military expeditions and raids to expand the range of influence of Islam. With Muhammad's death they took center stage, and their characters began more fully to form the ideal of the Quranic generation.

## 2. The Rightly Guided Caliphs

The first four successors of Muhammad as leaders of the Muslim community were Abu Bakr, Umar, Uthman bin Affan, and Ali bin Ibn Ali Talib. They are called by Muslims the "Rightly Guided Caliphs" because their leadership exhibited the fundamental qualities of: consensus and consultation in leadership (*ijma* and *shura*), allegiance of the community (*bay'a),* unity of the *ummah,* fidelity to the Muhammadan pattern (as opposed to *bid'ah* or innovation), piety (*iman*), and equality. For followers of Ali three of these Caliphs were tolerated usurpers. When Ali eventually came to power it realized the ideal of *näss,* or succession of the true leader of the Muslims, or *Imam,* through the passing on of the prophetic charisma within Muhammad's family. Ali's rule ended in 661 with his death in the midst of civil war. Islam was divided forever after between the followers of Mu'awiyah of the Umayyad family and those of Ali. It was a division that would ultimately give birth to the Sunni and Shī'ite Muslim communities.

*The Rightly Guided Caliphs were:*

*Abu Bakr (632–634 CE)*

*Umar (634–644 CE)*

*Uthman bin Affan (644–656 CE)*

*Ali bin Ibn Ali Talib (656–661 CE)*

### 632–634 CE, Abu Bakr

Abu Bakr, the first successor to Muhammad, began his rule in what would eventually be seen as ideal, and precedent-setting, circumstances. Upon the death of Muhammad, he urged the position as head of the community on others but accepted the role when the leading followers of Muhammad unanimously selected him (demonstrating the ideals of consultation, *shura*, and consensus, *ijma)* and the entire community swore an oath of allegiance (*bay'a).* For *sunni* Muslims this became the ideal for political leadership. His policy of distinguishing his private wealth as ruler from the public treasury and insisting that all Muslims shared in the spoils of war were exemplary of the ideals of financial integrity and just treatment of a united *ummah.* Sufi traditions maintain that he was one who met with Muhammad to hear esoteric teaching and meditate, and thus became the first founder of Islamic esotericism and mysticism.

He immediately faced a challenge to the unity of the Muslim community. At the end of Muhammad's life virtually all of the Arab tribes had embraced Islam. Many, however, saw themselves as personally loyal to Muhammad, not Allah or the abstract principle of Islam. In the first apostasy wars Abu Bakr reasserted Muslim control of Arab tribes and established Islam in Oman, Yemen, and Hadhramaut. He also confirmed the Quranic principle that Islam was a way of life commanded by Allah, not loyalty to a particular leader or teacher. Once embraced it could not be cast off. In 633 he sent military expeditions into Syria and Iraq and by July of 634 his forces had defeated the Byzantines and controlled Palestine. This first defeat of the great Christian empire stands for many Muslims as proof that Islam is the replacement for Christianity in God's plan.

## 634–644 CE, Umar

Umar's decisive campaign against the Sassanids in 635 began the permanent conquest of Iraq (the Tigris-Euphrates valley) and the fall of the ancient Christian center Ctesiphon in 637. After this Arab armies ranged eastward across all of Iran, and Islam displaced a second great empire, Persia, and its Zoarastrian religion. In 638 he completed the conquest of Syria and began the conquest of Egypt. Alexandria fell in 641. Such victories, and those which followed, helped define the Quranic promises that Muslims would be "winners" and enjoy success in this life and the hereafter.

In addition to his conquests Umar began to establish fundamental policies in relation to non-Muslims. He kept troops out of newly conquered cities because of their corrupting influence and instead established military cities (Basrah, Kufah, Jabiyah, Ramlah, and Fustat, or Cairo).

He also made the first treaties with non-Muslims living within Muslim-controlled territories. These became, for subsequent generations, the ideal of tolerance for minorities under an Islamic government. In much of Syria the Christian Monophysites, who had been suppressed by Byzantine Orthodoxy, welcomed the Muslim armies as liberators. It is for Muslims a further proof of this ideal. At the same time, Umar declared that Arabia was a holy land, and forced all non-Muslims to migrate. This established the purity of Islam's most sacred places and rituals. In 644 Umar was stabbed by a slave over a personal grudge. He was able, before he died, to appoint six leading men to choose his successor, confirming the ideal of consultation and election for a proper succession.

## 644–656 CE, 'Uthman ibn Affan

Uthman continued the military expansion of Islamic realms, developing the first Muslim navy and raiding into Tunisia. He also encouraged raids into Asia Minor, Armenia, and farther and farther east. As Muslim armies conquered new lands he initiated the policies that shaped Muslim life. It was under him that Quranic law was interpreted to give right on inheritance to wives and minor children. He also, in key Muslim centers, oversaw the standardization of the written Quran and established the seven official spoken versions corresponding to the pronunciation of Arabic.

It was also in his time that civil war again broke out among Muslims. The followers of Abu Bakr, 'Umar, and 'Ali, the son-in-law of the Prophet, made up a party of those closest to Muhammad himself when he lived. 'Uthman, however, was a member of the Umayyad family, a rival party. It had persecuted the first Muslims before converting to Islam. In 'Uthman's reign he greatly strengthened family power by appointing relatives to high posts and governorships. A third group of rebels was made of the unaffiliated Arab soldiers who had little unity, but could easily become discontented and swayed against particular leaders. Eventually the first and third of these groups began open rebellions against 'Uthman's rule. Their grievances were based on his policy of distributing conquered lands to established Muslim families rather than the soldiers who had conquered them, as well as charges of corruption.

Despite these political realities, acknowledged by Muslim historians, the focus of many Muslims in evaluating 'Uthman's failings is his enlargement of the *Ka'bah* (the sacred shrine in the middle of Medina) and his loss of the Prophet Muhammad's signet ring. Religious ideals are threatened most by the destruction of religious symbols. Despite these failings, 'Uthman is honored because he refused to allow an army to be raised to defend him when Medina was surrounded by rebels in 655. His patience with the rebels was not rewarded, and in 656 the rebels stormed the palace and killed him. Abu Bakr's son struck the first blow. The golden age of Islam was coming to an end.

## 656–661 CE, Ali ibn Ali Talib

Ali, raised by the rebels as the next leader of the Muslims, symbolized the end of the era when military and political leaders would also be seen as saints. He was known both as a chivalrous soldier and a religious mystic who, like Abu Bakr, passed on to future generations *tasawwuf*, or esoteric teachings from Muhammad. A story is told of how he once refused to kill an enemy because his motivation would have been personal anger rather than a defense of Islam. Many of his followers believed that Ali should have followed Muhammad as Caliph, based on the idea of spiritual succession (*näss*) within members of the Prophet's immediate family. For this group, who would become the *Shiites*, Ali's spiritual status outweighed all other considerations.

---

*Timeline of Early Muslim History*

*632: Death of the Prophet Muhammad. Election of Abu Bakr as the Caliph.*

*634: Death of Abu Bakr. Umar becomes the Caliph.*

*635: Conquest of Damascus.*

*637: Conquest of Syria. Fall of Jerusalem.*

*642: Conquest of Egypt.*

*643: Conquest of Azarbaijan.*

*644: Death of Umar. Othman becomes the Caliph.*

*647: Conquest of the island of Cypress.*

*656: Death of Othman. Ali becomes the Caliph. Battle of the Camel.*

*657: Ali shifts the capital from Madina to Kufa. Battle of Siffin.*

*659: Conquest of Egypt by Mu'awiyah.*

*660: Ali recaptures Hijaz and Yemen from Mu'awiyah. Mu'awiyah declares himself as the Caliph at Damascus.*

*661: Death of Ali. Accession of Hasan and his abdication. Mu'awiyah becomes the sole Caliph, founds Umayyad dynasty.*

Yet as a general and politician Ali was too often indecisive and weak. Mua'wiyyah, who came from the same family as 'Uthman, sought to avenge 'Uthman's death by wresting control of the Muslim community from Ali. Ali first compromised with him, seeking to preserve the peace, but was seen by some Muslims (particularly the community called *Kharijites)* as compromising the faith. Ali was forced into battle against them, widening the division among Muslims into three factions. Although the *Kharijites* were defeated militarily Ali was not able to conclusively defeat Mua'wiyyah. In 661, after Mua'wiyyah had been declared Caliph in Jerusalem, Ali agreed to withdraw his claim to the Caliphate in order to preserve the unity of the *ummah.* However, a member of the *Kharijite* party assassinated him. Mua'wiyyah went on to establish a family dynasty, overthrowing the ideals of consultation and consensus.

## 3. End of the Age

The rise of the Umayyad dynasty, and the defeat of Ali, ended the Golden Age of political consensus and unity among Muslims. It also meant the fracturing of the Muslim community along political, theological, and geographical lines. The withdrawal of the *Kharijites* (who fled to southern Arabia and settled) marked the first creation of a divided *ummah.* Then a few years after the death of Ali in 670 his son Hasan, who had already capitulated to Mua'wiyyah, was poisoned, supposedly by his wife who wanted to marry Yazid, Mua'wiyyah's son. Ali's other son, Husayn, tried to launch a revolt against Yazid when he became caliph in 680. Husayn, with nearly 100 of his relatives and family, were massacred by Yazid at the plain of Karbala in Iraq. His followers continued to believed that the only legitimate line of caliphs was from Muhammad through Ali to Hasan and Husayn and on to other direct descendants of the Prophet himself. But their differences were not merely political. The Shiites also developed a distinctive theology of spiritual authority and traditions of esoteric spirituality. Although persecuted under the Umayyads, they managed to continue, largely based in Iran and southern Iraq, until today they make up 20 percent of the Islamic world.

## 4. Modern Assessments of the Golden Age

The personalities and events of the first generation of Muslims have shaped individual Muslim lives and also the development of Muslim society. For Sunni Muslims the political and legal precedents set by Muhammad and the first four caliphs became the norm for subsequent Muslim societies. The authority of that generation would be enshrined as a basic principle of Islamic law.

For the Shī'ite community the betrayal and martyrdom of Ali, Hassan, and Hussein would become a dominant spiritual motif, reenacted yearly in a flood of religious emotion during the *Ashura* festival. The belief that only true leader of the Muslim community would come from this family line has inspired a kind of eschatological hope directed to the return of the final living successor of Muhammed. To be revealed at the final judgment, the *Imam al-Mahdi* will restore the fortunes of the true Muslim community. In the meantime renowned religious leaders (*ayatollah*) are believed to continue to have access to hidden knowledge previously mediated by the succession of descendants of Ali.

In the last 200 years the importance of the ideal of the *Salafiyya*, or "fathers," the Quranic generation and rightly guided caliphs, has been seen in a new light. Even before the colonial era this generation had inspired reformers such as Ibn Taymiyyah (1263–1328). He sought to cut beneath the accretions of extra-Islamic customs he thought had become part of the Islamic legal and theological tradition. He wished to restore the role of *ijithād* or independent reasoning in both criticizing the tradition and in developing a purer form of Islam in line with that of the first four caliphs.

As more and more Muslim societies came under the influence, and ultimately domination of European powers, their leaders began to search for ways to reconstruct and renew Islamic society. In the first generation of

Muslims they found long-neglected models for Muslim life, and a period in which the development of society was based on a continual process of reasoning from the principles of the Quran and Hadith, rather than application of a static legal tradition. The divisions that mark much of Muslim political opinion today spring in part from the different ways in which the ideal of the rightly guided caliphs is appropriated and applied.

## The Wahhabis

Muhammad ibn Abd al-Wahhab (1703–1792) lived in various parts of Arabia, Iraq, and Iran. Inspired in part by the writings of Ibn Taymiyyah, in 1763 he began actively preaching against the *Sufi* mystic movements and wrote his work *Kitab at-tawhīd* ("Book of Unity"). When he was expelled from his home city he settled in Ad-Dir'iyah, capital of Ibn Sa'ud's territories in Arabia. He would go on the provide the ideological motive for Ibn Sa'ud's conquest of the holy cities of Mecca and Medina, and the rule over Ibn Sa'ud's successors over what became Saudi Arabia. Through this political alliance, and control of the pilgrimage center of Mecca, al-Wahhab was able to both implement his ideas within the heart of Islam, and spread them to its farthest bounds as pilgrims returned to their homes. With the twentieth century discovery of oil in Saudi Arabia, vast financial resources became available to propagate Wahhabi doctrine and support Wahhabi teachers and movements around the world.

The center of al-Wahhab's teaching was a rejection of all innovations in Islamic doctrine or practice beyond the time of the Prophet, and a return to the purity of Islam in the first generation. To Wahhab what was at stake was nothing less than the unity of God, the central teaching of Islam. Restoring this teaching meant a critical reevaluation of the Muslim legal tradition based on a literal interpretation of its sources in the Quran and Hadith. Although he attacked what he saw as the innovations, his call for a literal interpretation of the Quran and Hadith, as well as a return to the purity of early Islam, was itself a novelty in Islamic history.

His teaching was rejected by traditionalist Muslim leaders who saw the rich diversity of Muslim civilization and its legal tradition as a reflection of the teaching of the Quran, and certainly not a perversion of it. Yet half a century after his death a new generation of Muslim reformers would also argue that a central aspect of Muhammad's teaching, and the practice of the

Quranic generation, was a process of continually applying the Quran and Hadith in new ways to new situations.

## The Traditionalists

The traditionalist opponents of al-Wahhab had originally exiled him from his home city. Generations of their followers across the Islamic world would oppose Wahhabism. They saw the time of Muhammad and the rightly guided caliphs through the lens of a rich, complex Islamic legal tradition and the glory of a world-spanning Islamic civilization. For the most part the traditionalists are *ulama,* or religious teachers who for over a thousand years have applied and passed on the legal and theological tradition of Islam's first centuries. It is a tradition that was largely fixed by the eleventh century CE, when the *ulama* reached a consensus that all of the implications of Quranic teaching and the Hadith had been fully worked out. It was a tradition that integrated local customs, the mystic tradition, and the insights of Greek philosophy into its law, spirituality, and metaphysics.

It is tempting for Westerners imbued with a love of progress to see the traditionalists merely as opponents of change who did not want to see their well-entrenched positions in Muslim societies threatened by puritan literalists like al-Wahhab. Yet they have also played an important role in preserving more than just an ancient legal and theological tradition. The Nahdlatul ulama is the largest Muslim organization in the world, with a membership of over 16 million Indonesian Muslims. It was formed as a traditionalist reaction to both the influence of Wahhabism and modernism in twentieth-century Indonesia. Its popularity developed because in defending traditional Islam it defended the indigenous Indonesian culture and cultural values that were integrated into that tradition.

The Islamic tradition has often been a tradition of embracing and transforming local spiritualties. It was precisely this accommodation of non-Arab and pre-Islamic spiritualties that al-Wahhab opposed, and that the traditionalists have maintained. Like both the Puritans and Reformers, the traditionalists hold that the Quran and Hadith are the sole sources of the Islamic religion, and idealize the first generation of Muslims. Yet for them the timelessness and universality of Islam are not found by reducing the religion to these sources, but in its actual success as a civilization and way of life over centuries. In this assessment the first modern Muslim reformers would not disagree, although they felt this tradition had also become a burden.

## Al Afghani and Muslim Reform

While al-Wahhab had been inspired toward reform by what he saw as heterodoxy within Islamic society, Jamal al Din al Afghani (1838–1897) was moved by the weakness of Islamic society in the face of European colonialism. He saw the debilitating effect of Western power on young Muslims, and the inability of Muslim leaders and societies to resist it. In his writings and speeches, he sought to remind Muslims of the revealed mandate and mission of Islam, and the glory of Islamic civilization. Like the traditionalists he maintained that Islam was a comprehensive way of life embracing politics, the social order, and worship. Yet he also believed Islam was a religion of change and progress, and of reason and action.

When Afghani looked at the *salafiyyah* or first generation of Muslims he saw men and women who reasoned from the Quran and Hadith in new and creative ways to develop Islamic society. Like Taymiyyah centuries earlier he called for renewal through *ijithad*. Yet he was not interested in a return to the original patterns of Muslim society. Rather al-Afghani maintained that in a constantly changing social environment *ijithad* should never cease. Islamic law was not a formal system of logical deductions from first principles that reached its limits in the eleventh century CE. It was a faithful response by each generation to the challenge of submission to God in fidelity to the Quran and Prophet. Al Afghani and those who followed him (such as Muhammad Abduh and Rashid Ridah) held up the ideal of the Quranic generation and maintained that in its *method* was the secret of renewal.

Since the time of Al Afghani, Muslim reform movements have moved in several directions—unified by their insistence on the necessity of *ijithad*. Sayyid Qutb (1906–1966) was the radical ideologue of the early Muslim Brotherhood and is regarded by many as the inspiration for the ideology of modern Muslim radicalism. He stressed that the Quranic generation was the locus in which Muslims discovered God's method of implementing Islam. And it was the period in which Islam overcame the forces of ignorance to establish God's way for humanity. For Qutb, Islam begins with the total transformation of the soul when a person submits to the truth that there is only one God, Allah, and that Muhammad is his Prophet. Islamic society arose organically among those who first completely submitted in this way.[2] He rejected contemporary Muslim society as just another form of the pre-Islamic *jahiliyya*, or ignorance, because it had lost this Quranic spirit and forgotten the Quranic method. Thus, for Qutb, *jihad*, or struggle, including violent struggle against their own supposed leaders, was to be expected by Muslims seeking to be faithful to the ideal of the first generation.

A far different voice is that of Zaiuddin Sardar (b. 1951), a Pakistani writer whose books have been influential in both Europe and Southeast Asia. Sardar wants the Muslim community to appropriate a method of reasoning that goes beyond a personal appropriation of the *shahada*. He sees in the development of Islamic law, including the principle of *ijithad*, a method that can be applied in each new situation in order continually to form and reform Islamic society. Unlike Qutb, who saw the Quranic generation as a time of life-or-death conflict with the forces of ignorance, Sardar and others like him see it as a period in which Muslims formulated an open, tolerant, and progressive civilization that was faithful both to God and the diversity of God's creation. For Sardar the governing principles established by Muhammad in Medina, the treaties he and the first caliphs made with non-Muslims, and the development of classical Islamic law and theology all reveal the method of reasoning by which the Quran and Hadith become the source of Muslim civilization.

Sardar's approach, which is found among many moderate Muslim reformers, leaves ample room for debate. In part this is a debate over exactly where the development of classical Islamic legal reasoning leaves off and the beginning of static Islamic law begins. In part it is a debate over which period in the first generation of Muslims sets the most useful precedent for modern Muslims. As Muslims wrestle with the issue of how a truly Islamic state should be formed they debate whether Muhammad's experience leading the first converts in Mecca, his treaty with the tribes of Medina, or perhaps the treaty of Umar with the non-Muslim groups in Palestine should be the model. And some argue that Muslims living as minorities in dominantly non-Muslim societies need to see Muhammad's treaty with the Abyssinian king as an example of the principles for Muslim life.[3]

---

2. Qutb, *Milestones*, 13–14.

3. Ramadan, *To Be a European Muslim*, 124.

## The Modernists

Among those who believe that Islam must be reformed in light of its existing situation are those who are truly *modern* in the sense that they seek to highlight in Islam values that are universal and independent of historical context. For these modernists Islam is compatible, and even enhanced by, modern social and political movements. The Quranic generation is no different from every succeeding generation, as every Muslim can relate to the timeless spirituality of the Quran.

Perhaps the most radical of such modernists was Kemal Ataturk, the founder of modern Turkey. He insisted on a thoroughly Westernized and secularized government and society. Symbols of Islam's historical and cultural peculiarity were banned from national life, and the Roman rather than Arabic alphabet was used to write the Turkish language. Islam was to be a private religion, supported for the sake of its universal moral and spiritual relevance rather than its role in politics and law. Other modernists have, like Ataturk, stressed nationalism in reforming the lives of Muslims and Islamic society. The eternal and timeless aspects of the religion are preserved in private religion, while indigenous culture and secular ideologies become the foundation for the development of society, whether national or worldwide.

Modernist and nationalist movements have played an important role in developing modern Muslim states from North Africa all the way to Indonesia. Within them Muslims have embraced the range of modern political ideologies, from communism to socialism to free market capitalism. While bitterly opposed by Islamicist movements, they still provide the dominant ideology in countries like Syria, Turkey, and Indonesia. Yet in other countries where modernist and nationalist Islam once prevailed, such as Iraq, Libya, Egypt, and the Central Asian republics, Islamist groups like the Taliban, al-Qaeda, and ISIS have destabilized and even demolished nationalist governments, throwing significant parts of the Muslim world into political turmoil.

## 5. Conclusion

For many Christians the disentangling of religion from the power of the state is one of the great achievements of the modern world. It has created a historically unparalleled tolerance of religious diversity and freedom of conscience. Although the separation of church and state is relatively new in Western history, it is not difficult to reconcile with the ideals of religious life pictured in the New Testament, which is a record of a tiny religious minority living in the midst of the Roman state.

For Muslims it has become clear in recent decades that secularist or nationalist movements are emotionally and spiritually disconnected from many, if not the majority, in their understanding of Islam. Across the Islamic world popular political movements based on specifically Muslim principles are growing stronger. However much the Quranic generation might be admired for its piety and spirituality, its political and military achievements remain equally an ideal to be emulated.

## Guide for Further Study

Review the key themes of the chapter. If members of the study group have questions about the these key themes it would be good to discuss these first.

### Key Themes

- The first generation of leaders provides models, both to be emulated and avoided, for Muslim life.

- The authority of the existing Quran and Sunnah rests in part on the fidelity of the first generation of Muslim leaders.

- The rightly guided caliphs set the basic patterns for Muslim political leadership and social and political structures.

- Some modern reform movements assume that Muslims must faithfully recreate this period politically, religiously, economically, and socially.

- Others see this period as an example of fidelity rather than a fixed pattern of Muslim life.

- All Muslims are inspired by the success of the first generation in achieving their own independence and spreading Islam across a vast territory. Many believe they can imitate this success in our time.

## Final Discussion Questions

- In the various readings we have seen that the first followers of Muhammad are idealized in different ways: as men who refused to innovate from the religion given by Muhammad, as men whose lives were molded directly by the Quran, as men who governed according to Muhammad's examples and precepts, and as a woman closest to the Prophet's heart. How are Christian attitudes toward the first followers of Jesus similar and different?

- Muslims frequently discuss how to best emulate the piety and success of the first followers of Muhammad. How have Christians tried to emulate the piety of the first followers of Jesus?

- Islam is divided into two major groups. The Sunni Muslims believe that the "Rightly Guided Caliphs" ended with Ali, but that the Islamic community went on to greater and greater achievements. Shī'ite Muslims remember the martyrdom of Ali's sons Hassan and Hussein, and the long period of persecution which followed. What do Christians believe is most important about the early Christian era? How do Christians measure success? What is the value of martyrdom for Christians?

- How do Christian interpretations of the first generation of the church compare with those of Muslims?

- Why is the first generation so important for both religions?

- Is it possible to understand either the Bible or the Quran without learning how the first readers and hearers understood them?

- What issues did the early Christian community share in common with the first Muslim community? In what ways were they different?

- In what ways should modern Christians draw inspiration from the generation of the apostles? How does that differ from the inspiration Muslims draw from their first generation?

## Additional Readings

In the two readings which follow, one by a radical Muslim politician and the other by a much more mainstream Islamic group in an American university, demonstrate the way in which Muslim piety is shaped by respect for the first generation of Muslims.

Qutb, Sayyid. *Milestones*. Indianapolis: American Trust, 1990.

### Excerpts from Chapter 1

1. At one time this Message created a generation without any parallel in the history of Islam, even in the entire history of man, the generation of the Companions of the Prophet (may Allah be pleased with them). After this, no other generation of this caliber was ever again to be found. It is true that we do find some individuals of this caliber here and there in history, but never again did a great number of such people exist in one region as was the case during the first period of Islam. . . .

    The spring from which the Companions of the Prophet, peace be on him, drank was the Noble Quran and only the Quran, since the Hadith of the Prophet, Peace be on him, and his teachings were an offshoot of this fountainhead. When someone asked the Mother of the Faithful, 'Aisha, may Allah be pleased with her, about the character of the Prophet, peace he on him, she answered, "His character was the Quran." Those of the first generation did not approach the Quran for the purpose of acquiring culture and information, nor for the purpose of taste or enjoyment. None of them came to the Quran to increase his knowledge for the sake of knowledge itself or to solve some scientific or legal problems, or to improve his understanding. Rather he turned to the Quran to find out what the Almighty Creator has prescribed for him and for the group in which he lived, for his life, and for the life of the group. . . .

    Thus they clearly realized that every moment of their lives was under the continuous guidance and direction of the Almighty Creator and that they were traversing the path of life under the wings of Allah's mercy. Because of this sense of constant relationship with Allah, their lives were molded in the sacred pattern that He Himself had chosen for them.

    When a person embraced Islam during the time of the Prophet, peace be on him, he would straightway cut himself off from *jahiliyyah*. . . .

Today too we are surrounded by *jahiliyyah*. Its nature is the same as during the first period of Islam, and it is perhaps a little more deeply entrenched. Our whole environment, people's beliefs and ideas, habits and art, rules and laws is *jahiliyyah*, even to the extent that what we consider to be Islamic culture, Islamic sources, Islamic philosophy, and Islamic thought are also constructs of *jahiliyyah*! This is why the true Islamic values never enter our hearts, why our minds are never illuminated by Islamic concepts, and why no group of people arises among us equal to the caliber of the first generation of Islam.

2. We must return to that pure source from which the first generation derived its guidance, free from any mixing or pollution . . .

Our primary purpose is to know what way of life is demanded of us by the Quran, the total view of the universe that the Quran wants us to have, the nature of Allah, taught to us by the Quran, the kind of morals and manners enjoined by it, and the kind of legal and constitutional system it asks us to establish in the world.

We know that in this we will have difficulties and trials, and we will have to make great sacrifices. But if we are to walk in the footsteps of the first generation of Muslims, through whom Allah established His system and gave victory over *jahiliyya*, the Allah must be the master of our wills. (pp. 11–16)

## Additional Questions

- For Qutb the Quran is the source of the greatness of the first generation of Muslims. What made the apostles of Jesus different from other generations?

- Qutb uses the word *jahiliyyah* (ignorance) to characterize both the society in Muhammad's time, and modern societies. How would a Christian characterization of modern society be different?

- For Qutb there is no progress in religion from the time of Muhammad to the present. Would you agree?

## The Rightly Guided Caliphs

This document was produced by the National Muslim Student Association of the USA and Canada, and is found on the Muslim Student Association of USC website (http://www.usc.edu/dept/MSA/politics/firstfourcaliphs. html).

## Meaning of the Word 'Caliph'

1. The word 'Caliph' is the English form of the Arabic word 'Khalifa,' which is short for **Khalifatu Rasulil-lah**. The latter expression means **Successor to the Messenger of God**, the Holy Prophet Muhammad (peace be on him). The title *'Khalifatu Rasulil-lah'* was first used for Abu Bakr, who was elected head of the Muslim community after the death of the Prophet.

## The Significance of the Caliphate

2. The mission of Prophet Muhammad (peace be on him), like that of the earlier messengers of God, was to call people to the worship of and submission to the One True God. In practice, submission to God means to obey His injunctions as given in the Holy Quran and as exemplified by Sunnah (the practice of the Prophet). As successor to the Prophet, the Caliph was the head of the Muslim community and his primary responsibility was to continue in the path of the Prophet. Since religion was perfected and the door of Divine revelation was closed at the death of the Prophet, the Caliph was to make all laws in accordance with the Quran and the Sunnah. He was a ruler over Muslims but not their sovereign since sovereignty belongs to God alone. He was to be obeyed as long as he obeyed God. . . .

## The Rightly-Guided Caliphs (Al-Khulafa-ur-Rashidun)

3. Those Caliphs who truly followed in the Prophet's foot steps are called 'The Rightly-Guided Caliphs' (Al-Khulafa-ur Rashidun in Arabic). They are the first four Caliphs: Abu Bakr, 'Umar, Uthman and Ali. All four were among the earliest and closest Companions of the Prophet (peace be on him). They lived simple and righteous lives and strove

MUSLIM FAITH AND VALUES

hard for the religion of God. Their justice was impartial, their treatment of others was kind and merciful, and they were one with the people—the first among equals. After these four, the later Caliphs assumed the manners of kings and emperors and the true spirit of equality of ruler and ruled diminished to a considerable extent in the political life of Muslims.

It should be clearly understood that the mission of Prophet Muhammad (peace be on him), and hence that of the Rightly-Guided Caliphs, was not political, social or economic reform, although such reforms were a logical consequence of the success of this mission, nor the unity of a nation and the establishment of an empire, although the nation did unite and vast areas came under one administration, nor the spread of a civilization or culture, although many civilizations and cultures developed, but only to deliver the message of God to all the peoples of the world and to invite them to submit to Him, while being the foremost among those who submitted.

## What About the Present?

4. The primary responsibility of an Islamic government is still the same as it was in the days of the early Caliphs: to make all laws in accordance with the Quran and the Sunnah, to make positive efforts to create and maintain conditions under which it will be possible and easy for Muslims to live an Islamic life, to secure impartial and speedy justice for all, and to strive hard in the path of God. Any government which is committed to such a policy is truly following the message delivered by the Prophet (peace be on him).

(*The document then gives a lengthy history of the first four Caliphs.*)

## Conclusion

5. With the death of Ali, the first and most notable phase in the history of Muslim peoples came to an end. All through this period it had been the Book of God and the practices of His Messenger—that is, the Quran and the Sunnah—which had guided the leaders and the led, set the standards of their moral conduct and inspired their actions. It was the time when the ruler and the ruled, the rich and the poor,

the powerful and the weak, were uniformly subject to the Divine Law. It was an epoch of freedom and equality, of God-consciousness and humility, of social justice which recognized no privileges, and of an impartial law which accepted no pressure groups or vested interests.

## Additional Questions

- What was the mission of Muhammad and the rightly guided Caliphs?
- Can a modern political leader undertake such a mission?
- Would modern people ever willingly subject themselves to what Muslims regard as divine law?

## The Poetry of Iqbal

Muhammad Iqbal was an influential nineteenth-century Muslim reformer from India. This tribute to Fatima draws on her relationship to both Muhammad, Ali, and her sons to give a feminine aspect to Muslim spirituality, and a model for Muslim womanhood.

### Iqbal, Muhammad. "That the Lady Fatima is the Perfect Pattern of Muslim Womanhood." http://www.geocities.com/ahlulbayt14/poems.html.

> Mary is hallowed in one line alone,
> That she bore Jesus; Fatima in three,[4]
> For that she was the sweet delight of him
> Who came a mercy to all living things,
> Leader of former as of latter saints,
> Who breathed new spirit into this dead world
> And brought to birth the age of a New Law.
> His lady she, whose regal diadem
> God's words adorn Hath there come any time,
> The chosen one, resolver of all knots
> And hard perplexities, the Lion of God,
> An emperor whose place was a hut,
> Accoutered with one sword, one coat of mail.

4. Fatima was the daughter of the Holy Prophet Muhammad, the wife of Imam Ali, and the mother of Imam Hasan and Imam Husain.

And she his mother, upon whom revolves
Love's compasses, the leader of Love's train,
That single candle in the corridor
Of sanctity resplendent, guardian
Of the integrity of that best race
Of all God's peoples; who, that the fierce flame
Of war and hatred might extinguished be
Trod underfoot the crown and royal ring
His mother too, the lord of all earth's saints
And strong right arm of every freeborn man,
Husain, the passion in the song of life,
Teacher of freedom to God's chosen few.
The character, the essential purity
Of holy children from the mothers come.
She was the harvest of the well-sown field
Of self-surrender, to all mothers she
The perfect pattern, Fatima the chaste.
Her heart so grieved, because one came in need,
She stripped her cloak and sold it to a Jew;
Though creatures all, of light alike and fire,
Obeyed her bidding, yet she sank her will
In her good consort's pleasure. Fortitude
And meekness were her schooling; while her lips
Chanted the Book, she ground the homely mill.
No pillow needed she to catch her tears,
But wept contrition's offering of pearls
Upon the skirt of prayer; which Gabriel stooped
To gather, as they glistened in the dust,
And rained like dew upon the Throne of God.
God's Law a fetter of locks about my feet
To guard secure the Prophet's high behest,
Else had I surely gone about her tomb
And fallen prostrate, worshipping her dust.

## Additional Questions

- What women have been important models for Christians?
- How are they similar, and different from, Fatima?

# Chapter 6: The Shari'a and Civilization

In the year 2001 in the Kaduna state of northern Nigeria riots broke out. The state government had announced that it would make the revealed *shari'a* law of Islam the official law of the state. Some Muslim groups took the opportunity to enforce their idea of the *shari'a* by attacking Christian churches and businesses. Some Christian groups took to the streets in protest of what they believed diminished their rights as a religious minority. Since then violence has flared across Nigeria on a regular basis. Nor is Nigeria unique, with much of the Muslim world having experienced violence surrounding efforts to implement *shari'a*. whether by existing governments or opposition political movement promoting some form of Islamization that will restore the place of Islamic law (at least among Muslims) and the power and dignity of the Muslim community.

> *"The goal is not to know God, but to obey him perfectly. The devout do not love God's essence (dhat) but his command (shari'a)." Ibn Tamiyyah*

Within these movements the full implementation of *shari'a* has been both the symbol of a truly Islamic society and a panacea promising to cure all social and economic ills. Like all ideals and panaceas, it draws on many levels of the Muslim religious experience for its power. It can be seen as the articulation in daily life of the deepest and most fundamental Muslim beliefs. It can be seen as the source of Muslim political and social theory. It can embody the expansive glory of Islamic civilization. Or it can be seen as the irreducible core of authentic Muslim life. For some Muslims it plays all these roles and others as well.

## The Civilization of Islam

From the first Muslim conquests outside Arabia in the early seventh century to the middle of the tenth century, the Islamic world developed with an unprecedented vigor. Historians take note of the military accomplishments of the Muslim armies, which dominated virtually every force with which they came in contact. The Umayyad and Abbasid dynasties assimilated and developed upon the social and political institutions they absorbed until there existed a true empire stretching from Spain to Central Asia. Traders, intellectuals, bureaucrats, and religious teachers wove together a civilization yielding nothing to its illustrious predecessors. Its material wealth was so vast that one of its rulers could boast a carpet woven entirely of precious gems. Its merchants pioneered the use of letters of credit, bank notes, and universal trade regulations. Its thinkers and scientists preserved and improved upon the legacy of Greece and Rome to lay the foundations for modern mathematics, chemistry, astronomy, and physiology. The renaissance of Christian Europe would be ignited in part when Christians learned Arabic to have access to this civilization.

Yet by the mid-nineteenth century the Islamic civilization was little in evidence except through the beauty of its architecture. The last dynasty with some claim to an empire, the Ottomans, was crumbling, and the majority of Muslims lived under European colonial rule. Relative to Europeans most Muslims were impoverished, economically backward, and uneducated. Yet in addition to memories there remained at the core of Muslim life the *shari'a* as a reminder of and a call to greatness.

The root meaning of the word *shari'a* is a path or way leading to water, and you still see this meaning in modern Arabic. As it refers to God's command, God's way, it may be said to have been the path to Islamic civilization. From a historical standpoint its laws, its methods, and its institutions developed in tandem with the more complex historical processes that shaped the world of Islam. And from a religious standpoint *shari'a* could be seen as the basis for the civilization, discovered and articulated by the Muslim jurists even as Muslim rulers and generals were discovering the power of Islam to unite and convert humanity. For Muslim reformers the *shari'a* was the framework upon which Islamic civilization had been built, even as it was the path to paradise for each individual believer.

As modern Muslims have longed to restore or re-create that civilization it is natural that they have looked to the *shari'a* to provide a basis for their work. In theory the *shari'a* puts all relationships—family, social, economic, and political—into conformity with God's will. It guides husbands, wives, and children as they seek to build up loving and productive families. It insures that political structures embody the principles of God's justice and the unity of the *ummah*. It keeps the architect or urban planner on a path that reflects not only human creativity and ingenuity but glorifies God as well. It can be everything from the ideological basis of human society to a dress code for those whose aim is modesty. It regulates relations between Muslims and non-Muslims, between nations, between customers and vendors, and between teacher and pupil. Yet as the riots in Nigeria, protests in Malaysia and Pakistan, and political unrest in Indonesia show, restoring the Islamic civilization through implementing the *shari'a* is not universally welcomed or uniformly understood.

## The Development of the *Shari'a*

In the 1890s the Sultan of Trengganu, on the East Coast of the Malay Peninsula, rebelled against British colonialism. Faced with overwhelming military force, he appealed to the epitome of Muslim political and military power, the Ottoman Caliph in Istanbul. It was a naïve appeal, given that the Ottoman regime was crumbling.

A century later, Muslim politicians in the same state were fighting to keep political control out of the hands of the nationalist political party that controlled the federal government. They made a different kind of appeal to the power of Islam. To capture the hearts of the Muslim voters they promised to implement *shari'a* law as the law of the state. They won the state election, although they could not fulfill much of what they promised.

For those longing for an Islamic government the *shari'a* continues to have a universal moral authority, even as Muslims are politically and economically fragmented. For Muslims *shari'a* is the revelation of the Quran applied to human affairs, and the authority of the Prophet extended to address the political, social, and religious concerns of later generations of Muslims.

---

*Basic Concepts of Islamic Legal Development:*

*Quran—God's revelation to Muhammad, a fundamental source of legal reasoning.*

*Sunnah—The traditional sayings of Muhammad, of legal reasoning.*

*Qiyas—Application to new situations, by analogy, of legal reasoning.*

*Ijma*—*The consensus of learned jurists, of legal reasoning.*

*Ijtihad*—*Reasoning independent of tradition but not necessarily opposed to it.*

*Istihsan*—*The good of the community, a basis for deciding between different interpretations.*

*Ra'y*—*Personal judgment exercised in specific cases.*

The *shari'a,* as understood by most Muslims, is a large body of revealed laws "discovered" over a period of three centuries after the death of Muhammad. Initially the *shari'a* consisted of the legal regulations found in the Quran, supplemented and interpreted by Muhammad's words and actions. These two, the Quran and Sunnah, are the primary sources of the *shari'a.* After the death of Muhammad, the recognized religious leaders of different local communities faced the challenge of making legal rulings for situations not explicitly addressed in the Quran and Sunnah. In some cases they adopted local customary law when it was not in conflict with the Quran. In others they applied existing regulations to new situations by analogy. Some applied complex forms of legal reasoning as they tried to discern the underlying intention of the Quran and Sunnah *(ijithād).* Others accepted the principle that the good of the community determined the law *(istihsān).* While in the end they might rely on their personal judgment *(ra'y),* the most authoritative rulings were those accepted by a wide range of legal experts *(ijma).* Thus, the *shari'a* developed as these Muslim *jurists* (judges and legal experts) ruled on specific questions about how faithful Muslims should live.

Over time the judgments of the most famous experts were written down and circulated. These books of law *(fiqh)* were unlike modern laws passed by a legislature. Indeed in many cases the jurists were in determined opposition to the laws implemented by the political authorities. As a result, their *shari'a* has an authority independent of any Muslim government. This is why it is such an effective tool for either legitimating or opposing political power in the modern world. In the absence of a universally recognized Caliph, *shari'a* becomes the locus of all authority in Islam.

Three significant developments served to fix the content of the *shari'a* and confirm its divine authority. The first was the development of a science for collecting and evaluating traditions of the Prophet Muhammad. Experts in religious law traveled widely, collecting traditions from those most closely associated with Muhammad. They then gauged the authenticity of these traditions by finding how many different people knew the tradition, and how directly that knowledge came from the Prophet. Finally they recorded both the traditions and the evidence for their authenticity. Eventually there were widely accepted and circulated versions of the Sunnah. These allowed Muslim legal experts from across the Muslim world to have a common basis for their rulings.

The second development was the legal theory of Muhammad Ibn-Idris al-Shafi'i (767–820 CE), which served to further systematize and fix the legal tradition. Al-Shafi'i maintained that all Islamic law should be based on four "roots" (*usūl*). These were the Quran, the Sunnah, analogical reasoning (*qiyās*), and the consensus of past legal experts (*ijma*). He argued that these roots were revealed in the Quran itself.

Missing from his scheme was the role played in earlier years by customary law and the personal judgment of competent scholars. As al-Shafi'i's ideas became widely accepted, the development of Islamic law became more formulaic and consistent so that the results became more authoritative. The *shari'a* could truly be seen as Divine law because it was based on a *revealed method* applied to *revealed knowledge*.

Finally, by the middle of the tenth century, Muslim jurists would come to a consensus that given a limited body of revelation and of prophetic traditions, and a fixed method of interpretation, they had discovered in their books of *fiqh* all of God's law that it was possible for humans to know. The *shari'a* was complete, and all that remained was to imitate those who first discovered each rule and apply those rules in different situations.

---

*The Accepted Schools of Islamic Law*

*Sunni*

*Maliki after Malik ibn Anas (711–795 CE)*

*Hanbali after Ahmad ibn Hanbal, (780–855 CE)*

*al-Shafi'i after Ibn Idris al-Shafi'i (767–820 CE)*

*Hanifi after Abu Hanifa al-Numan (699–767 CE)*

*Shiite*

*Ja'fari after Ja'far al-Sadiq (702–765 CE)*

---

This does not mean that the *shari'a* was simple. The results of juristic activity over several centuries were not entirely uniform. There developed four basically regional Sunni "schools" of Islamic law (Maliki, Hanbali, al-Shafi'i, and Hanifi, each named after its most prominent jurist). Their rulings differed in part because early on they adopted different customary laws, in part because they took different approaches to interpreting the Quran (more or less literally), and in part because they made use of different collections of the Sunnah of the Prophet. Yet even with their differences these books of *fiqh* were regarded as Divine law, carrying the authority of the Quran and Prophet because they were in theory based directly on the Quran and Sunnah.

In the Twelver Shiite tradition, the school of law stemming from the work of Ja'far al-Sadiq, the sixth Imam, became dominant. With other schools of Shiite law it never accepted the idea that the possibility of *ijtihad* was closed, since living Shiite scholars continued to have spiritual access to the wisdom of the successors to Muhammad.

## The Books of Law

Within the books of law there was a wide range of material, and law is approached from many different standpoints. All the books make a fundamental distinction between duties toward God (*ibadat*) and duties toward others (*mu'amalat*.) The former includes all the regulations concerning the five pillars of Islam, including forms of prayer, fasting, pilgrimage, the *zakāt* tax, and any matter relating to human obligations to God. These were discussed in the first chapter.

The latter includes rules related to marriage and family relations (including provisions for divorce, determining custody of children, and inheritance), rules covering economic relations, social relations, and rules for states conducting international relations in peace and war.

It is an all-embracing system, *yet it is not complete*. It includes only such law as could be derived using the four *usūl* spelled out by al-Shafi'i. There were and are many areas, particularly in the governing of society at large and in complex business relations, where the *jurists* could not formulate what would be regarded as divine law according to their own principles. There were also many individual disputes they could not resolve because the rules of evidence specified in the *shari'a* were unobtainable.

For example, a verdict in certain cases required four male witnesses. Without such witnesses a judge bound to the *shari'a* could not rule on guilt or innocence. Like all judges, the Muslim jurists were careful to distinguish the circumstances in which their rulings were valid or invalid and as a result certain cases and types of cases were left to the political authorities. Thus, a distinctive branch of the *shari'a*, the *siyāsa shari'a*, emerged. The Caliphs and their subordinates made their own laws independent from but in harmony with *shari'a* proper, as well as having their own courts to try cases that could not be tried under the *shari'a*.

The distinction between the laws of the rulers (and their courts) and those of the Muslim *jurists* helped serve to maintain the purity, and authority, of the *shari'a*. Yet the conflict between the comprehensiveness claimed by the *shari'a* and the reality that societies changed and evolved under extra-*shari'a* guidance has made it difficult for modern Muslims to agree on what it means to implement this ideal in their own lives, and nations.

## The Shari'a and the Islamic State

In the nineteenth and twentieth centuries the existence of nation-states with fixed boundaries, stable constitutions, and more or less democratic governments came to be seen in the West as the proper successors to the older political order of kingdoms and empires. The process of forming new nation-states began in the sixteenth and seventeenth centuries, and continued into the twentieth century with the dissolution of the colonial empires of Britain, France, the Netherlands, the United States, and in recent years Russia.

For most Muslims these developments were warmly greeted. Like subjugated peoples of all religious persuasions, they were glad to be freed from colonial empires. They longed to live in a political context in which their values and ways of life, rather than those of their colonial masters, could have precedence. Yet Islam, and the *shari'a*, were often not given pride of place in the new Muslim states. In some countries (such as Indonesia and Malaysia) the role of Islam in government was intentionally limited in order to keep support of non-Muslim groups. In others Muslim leaders could not agree on what constituted the *shari'a* and how it should be implemented. In some cases, the dominant political ideology was communist, or nationalist, or secularist, and distinctly Islamic voices were excluded from the political arena.

As the twentieth century progressed, Muslims felt a growing gap between the high hopes accompanying political independence and the actual poverty and political oppression under which they lived. It was natural that the failure to create *Islamic* states should be blamed, and that political movements would arise promising to cure the ills of the nation through Islamization and the implementation of *shari'a* law. Such movements now exist in virtually every Muslim country, often claiming to represent a majority of Muslims simply on the basis of being "Islamic." Their future is uncertain, yet the challenges they face, and present, are shaping world politics.

## The Shari'a as a Guide to Government

As it touches upon government, the *shari'a* as it is found in the books of law is less a political theory than a collection of guidelines for Islamic government. Certain institutions, such as the courts presiding over cases in *shari'a* law (the *qādi* courts), government offices in charge of enforcing Muslim law, and institutions for collecting and distributing *zakāt*, as well as the Caliphate itself, were accepted and regulated. The *shari'a* also regulated relations with resident religious minorities based on Quran, Sunnah, and the agreements of the first Caliphs with their subjects.

A substantial body of law regulated international relations and guided the Caliphs in the making of both peace and war. Yet the *shari'a* was not a constitution, nor did it recognize the legitimacy of different competing or cooperating powers in human society. Power was assumed to originate with God. God's vice-regent, the Caliph, used it legitimately when he implemented divine law in his territories and carried out the duty of *jihad* to expand the realm of Islam.

Given the importance of the Caliph it is not surprising that the *shari'a* focused on the legitimate means by which a Caliph was chosen, and on carefully delineating his ideal character. While jurists were not uniform in their views, they generally agreed that the means by which he should ideally be chosen were those found in the first rightly guided Caliphs: nomination, consultation, consensus, and acceptance through an oath of loyalty. Recognizing the need for strength, some believed that seizing power by force might also be legitimate. In any case, once in power the Caliph was responsible only to God. The majority of jurists did not recognize the legitimacy of rebellion. As for qualifications, the jurists agreed that the Caliph should be a male Muslim of the bani-Quraish tribe (that of Muhammad) who was sane, learned in the law, pious, and physically capable of leading Muslim armies into battle.

Beyond these guidelines the *jurists* were primarily interested in the principles by which the Caliph governed. Two general principals applied: that the Caliph act in accordance with the *shari'a*, and that he consult with the jurists on all matters of law. Ideally the Caliph would employ a group of jurists for this purpose. The assumption of the jurists was that the *shari'a* discovered and codified by the four schools of law would cover the critical elements of human life, and that the Caliph would essentially fill in the gaps with his pious judgment until the ideal of Islam was realized throughout society.

This godly *ideal* of government and its leaders would dominate the Islamic political theory until 1924. In that year the last Ottoman Caliph was deposed when the modern Turkish state was formed. Since then there has been no universally recognized Caliph in the Muslim world, forcing Islamic political theory to evolve in many different directions. Since the end of the Caliphate Muslim political theorists have struggled to reach a consensus on how, or whether, government based on the godly ideal of *shari'a* can be rationalized with modern democratic principles.

## The Shari'a and International Relations

In the idealized world of revealed law, humanity was regarded as living within one of three realms: the *dar al-Islam* (or realm of Islam), the *dar al-Harb* (the realm of war), and the *dar al-Sul* (the realm of those at peace with, but not under Islam). In theory this last realm existed only as long as the first treaties of Muhammad with his non-Muslim neighbors. Regarding everything outside the realm of Muslim leadership as the "realm of war" emphasized the obligation of Muslim rulers to extend the realm of Islam. In the latter part of the twentieth century Muslim political theorists have sought to revive the idea of the *dar al-Sul*, in order to emphasize that most Muslims live in nations that have peaceful relations with the non-Muslim world.

The process of *jihad*, the struggle to enlarge the realm of Islam, was extensively regulated by classic *shari'a*. Islamic law stressed that *jihad* was a collective obligation initiated only by the Caliph, and condemned attacks on non-Muslims that were opportunistic or motivated by personal

grudges. Non-Muslims and their rulers were first to be persuaded to submit to Allah and Islamic rule. If this failed then they were to be offered an
opportunity to surrender and live under the Islamic law governing religious minorities. Only when this failed, or in situations where the realm
of Islam was under attack, should the Caliph launch an armed invasion of
non-Muslim territory.

Once at war the Caliph and his army were obliged to recognize and
protect non-combatants, treat captured prisoners with dignity, and protect
the property seized from their adversaries. In the most detailed books of
law these rules meticulously protect the rights of those caught up in war,
and in many respects were nearly a millennium ahead of the formulation
of the Geneva Convention. It needs to be remembered, however, that these
rules were not derived from a treaty between nations but were a moral obligation on Muslim rulers. Thus, there existed no means apart from God's
anticipated judgment on sinners to enforce them.

Eventually the jurists recognized that Muslim governments would
enter into peaceful relations with non-Muslim governments, and they discovered in the *shari'a* rules for making and keeping peace. Central to these
were guidelines for the making and keeping of treaties, so long as they were
regarded as temporary pauses in the mandated process of *jihad*. In general,
the *shari'a* holds treaties and contracts to be sacrosanct, and Caliphs and
military leaders were expected to keep their end of a treaty regardless of
failures by the other party—unless the *dār al-Islam* was threatened.

Again, however, the obligation of a Muslim ruler to abide by a treaty
was a moral obligation rooted in a Divine mandate, not a legal obligation
in international law. The *shari'a* recognizes no equality between nations
in international law. The Islamic state represents (at least in theory) Divine
law. All others exist in the realm that should and will eventually submit to
that law. Whether this is different from the moral superiority some Western nations assume for their understanding of democracy and human
rights is an open question.

This is perhaps the key feature of *shari'a* when applied to international relations. As an ideal of human unity under divine sovereignty,
Muslims regard it as *universal* rather than national or international. In
a world in which every human is morally obliged to follow it, but there
exists no leader legally responsible to enforce it, those who violate it may
do so with impunity. Non-Muslims might argue that this speaks to the
value of truly international agreements and international agencies such

as the UN that can enforce them. At least some Muslims would reply that it simply shows the need to once again make the *shari'a* the rule of law in Muslim lands, and for Muslim leaders to take up their moral obligation to enforce it universally.

## The Shari'a and Religious Minorities

Religious pluralism was characteristic of the earliest Muslim societies. Arab Jews and Christians lived side by side with their Arab Muslim neighbors, according to long-established customary law. These interreligious relationships first underwent a fundamental change when non-Muslims were expelled from the region around Mecca and Medina, and secondly when the expanding Islamic empire embraced substantial Christian and Jewish populations. The early Muslim Caliphs dealt with religious pluralism in part by establishing new Muslim cities to separate Muslims from the older Christian and Jewish populations, and in part by entering into treaties with the non-Muslim minorities.

The treaty of Umar, the first of these, became the center of *shari'a* law regarding religious minorities (see Appendix B). In general it granted non-Muslims permission to live under their traditional leaders and laws so long as they didn't violate Muslim law in public. It excused them from the obligations for taxes and military service enjoined on Muslims, while requiring that they pay a special tax for the privilege of living under Muslim rule. In a number of different ways, it specified that personally and as communities they should avoid being mistaken for Muslims and should publicly humble themselves in the presence of Muslims.

---

*The Treaty of Umar*

*"This is a writing to Umar from the Christians of such and such a city. When You [Muslims] marched against us [Christians]: we asked of you protection for ourselves, our posterity, our possessions, and our co-religionists; and we made this stipulation with you, that we will not erect in our city or the suburbs any new monastery, church, cell or hermitage; that we will not repair any of such buildings that may fall into ruins, or renew those that may be situated in the Muslim quarters of the town; that we will not refuse the Muslims entry into our churches either by night or by day; that we will open the gates wide to passengers and travellers; that we will*

*receive any Muslim traveller into our houses and give him food*
*and lodging for three nights; that we will not harbor any spy in our*
*churches or houses, or conceal any enemy of the Muslims. . . ."*

It is telling that in the *sharia* it is treaties that regulate non-Muslims. The Muslim jurists recognized that the *dār al-Islam* embraced many nations, some of which were geographically defined and others of which were defined by ethnicity, religion, or culture. The concept of a *state* with fixed boundaries and a *citizenship* with common rights and obligations was no more part of Islamic law than it was part of European law prior to the eighteenth century. But while pre-modern European law tended to divide the inhabitants of a realm into social classes with differing rights, privileges, and obligations, the *shari'a* divided the inhabitants of *dār al-Islam* according to their religious community.

The actual situation of the religious minorities under Muslim government varied dramatically. In some periods Christians and Jews played prominent roles in society and government and were fully integrated into important social organizations. Muslim rulers saw the presence of different communities in their cities as a symbol of wealth and blessing. In these times the more demeaning provisions of the *shari'a* tended to be set aside or reinterpreted. Muslim treatment of minorities could be seen as an ideal of toleration and mutual respect in a plural framework, a living example of God's intention that humanity be both one and varied. It is useful for Christians to remember that when the Jews were expelled from Christian Spain in 1492, and were persecuted in Christian Europe, they found a welcome and chance to prosper in Muslim lands.

Yet when Muslim governments were under financial or political stress they could find reason within the *shari'a* to burden and suppress religious minorities. This mixed legacy is a reason that in modern Muslim countries religious minorities are justifiably anxious about the implementation and imposition of the *shari'a*. More fundamentally they question whether the *sharia* can recognize *citizenship* rights within a modern state defined by geographical boundaries and living under laws that apply equally to all its inhabitants. For non-Muslims in Muslim lands toleration of minorities living circumscribed lives is not sufficient for the twenty-first century. They are demanding to be full, equal partners in the building of the modern states in which they live.

The most recent development in this aspect of *shari'ah* was a conference of Muslim religious leaders from across the members of the Organization of Islamic States in January of 2016 in Marrakesh, Morocco. The official declaration of the conference used the treaty Muhammad made with the times of Medina (called the Charter of Median) as a basis for reflection on an Islamic understanding of citizenship rights in a modern nation-state (see Appendix C).

It was groundbreaking in two ways; first in calling for new legal reasoning around the concept of citizenship as inclusive of diverse religious groups, and second in affirming that it is "unconscionable to employ religion for the purpose of aggressing upon the rights of religious minorities in Muslim countries." While such declarations do not change the reality of oppression of religious minorities in many Muslim nations, this particular declaration is a turning point in rejecting the legitimization of that oppression by the majority of the world's Muslims.

## Crime and Punishment

Rulers and governments from time immemorial have taken responsibility for both making law and also enforcing it. Yet the *shari'a* has a complex approach to law enforcement that only gives partial power to the state. The historical development of Islam led (as mentioned above) to a dual system of courts: the *qadi* courts (named for the presiding judge who was an expert in *shari'a* law) and the government courts. The *shari'a* was both the divine law of the *shari'a* courts and the divine law that recognized the need and legitimacy of the government courts.

Even within the *shari'a* proper there is a further distinction between crimes against God and crimes against persons. And for these two categories of crime three types of punishments are recognized: 1) those prescribed by God's law because God's rights have been violated, 2) those which are regulated by God's law but which arise because the rights of humans have been transgressed, and 3) those special measures that may be taken in the public interest against criminals whose actions have no punishment prescribed in the Quran and Hadith. The state has responsibility only for prosecuting crimes of the first and third type. The families and individuals afflicted are responsible for the prosecution of crimes of the second type.

*"Whoever turns back from his belief (is apostate), openly or secretly, take him and kill him wheresoever ye find them, like any other infidel. Separate yourself from him altogether. Do not accept intercession in his regard." (Al-Baidhawi, commentary on Surah 4:89)*

*"To everyone acquainted with Islamic law it is no secret that according to Islam the punishment for a Muslim who turns to kufr (infidelity, blasphemy) is execution." ("The Punishment of the Apostate according to Islamic Law" by Abul al a Mawdudi.)*

Crimes against God include not only failure to carry out the ritual requirements of Islam but also specific offenses against God's order. These are highway robbery or armed robbery (which were defined to include what in modern law are terrorist activities), adultery, consumption of alcohol, and apostasy. For each the Quran or Hadith provides a specific punishment: removal of feet for armed robbery, death by stoning for adultery (carried out by the witnesses to the act), whipping for alcohol consumption, and death for unrepentant apostates. The Quran also specifies the punishment for normal theft (cutting off of the hand) and slander (lashing), which are regarded as crimes against persons.

Crimes such as murder, bodily harm, and damage to property are considered in the *shari'a* to be affairs between the persons or families involved. The aggrieved parties would appeal to a court for a judgment of guilt, then the settlement could be agreed between the parties. In the cases of homicide and bodily harm it was up to the family to enforce the judgment, although appeal could be made to the local government for help.

A final category of crime and punishment is that broad group of offenses which are not specified in the Quran or Sunnah, or in which the evidence available does not meet *shari'a* court standards. A commonly prosecuted example of the former is "close proximity," which forbids men and women who are not related or married to be alone together. An example of the latter is a case of rape that cannot be prosecuted because there are no pious, male witnesses to the act itself.

When non-Muslims protest the severity of punishment specified by the *shari'a* its supporters point out that *shari'a* courts are encouraged to be lenient in their interpretation of the crime and strict in their demands for evidence. The legal traditions encourage judges to leave punishment of crimes against God up to God if at all possible. As a result, actual applications of *shari'a* punishments were less frequent and severe than the laws would make it appear.

More problematic is that the *shari'a* regulates behavior that modern Western nations regard as no business of either the state or the community. This includes such crimes as drinking alcohol, close proximity, apostasy, and failure to keep regulations concerning prayer and fasting. The ideal of Islamic law is that it is God's comprehensive rule for human life: actualized by God's vice-regent (Caliph) and the *jurists* in a society committed to Islam. The ideal of most Western democracies has been shaped by the assumption that human freedom and happiness is best secured when religion, and religious law, is isolated to the realm of private conviction. Islamic law is based on the idea that the government should protect its people from wrong belief while contemporary Western law is based on protecting the individual conscience from the government's interference. And in the modern West crimes and punishments are not divinely mandated, but come from rational human consideration of what is best for human society.

There is no easy compromise between these two understandings of the ideal of law.

## The Limits of the State in Islam

While *shari'a* claims to be absolute because it originates in divine revelation, it does not grant to the state nearly the powers assumed by most modern states. The *jurists* whose efforts gradually discovered and articulated the *shari'a* fiercely maintained their independence from control by the Caliphs or public opinion. In practice this meant the Caliph limited their power to the realms of family law, religious regulations, and enforcing personal contracts that were usually of little interest to the state. Modern theories of the Islamic state (such as that implemented in Iran) maintain that an independent body of jurists should have the final say over the actions of both the legislative and executive branches of government. And just as the Caliph could not infringe the rights of the independent jurists, so the jurists themselves were reluctant to infringe on the rights of men to rule their families, and families to settle internal disputes.

There is a great deal of difference between the absolutist governments of the Abbasid dynasty and Islamic civilization at its height, and those of the twentieth century. The absolute authority of the Caliph was best maintained when it was above most personal and political activities.

Modern absolutist states, on the other hand, maintain their authority by seeking to dominate all personal and political activities. And all modern states have far more power to influence the lives of their citizens than did the states of classical Islam.

The ideal state of the *sharia* deals with religious minorities by creating a social realm in which they maintain their own laws and customs. Modern states deal with religious minorities by allowing them freedom for private religious activities while insisting on their conformity with all other standards of behavior regulated by the state. And this influences Muslims living in the West. In the United States, for example, laws regulating marriage and divorce, humane treatment of animals, and dress for school children effectively prevent Muslims from following the *shari'a* with regard to polygamous marriage, ritual sacrifice, and the *hijāb* (clothing that covers the hair and entire body as mandated by the *sharia*.)

While non-Muslim minorities in Muslim lands fear that the implementation of *shari'a* will take away their rights as citizens, many Muslims find that citizenship in modern states intrudes upon their personal and community affairs in a way that prevents them from being fully *muslim*, fully submitting to divine law.

## The Shari'a and Economics

The earliest revelations of the Quran were directed at an Arab society obsessed with wealth and increasingly corrupt in its economic relations. The long Arab tradition of raiding caravans loaded with trade goods was not in question. Muhammad himself would lead such raids (against non-Muslims) to the end of his life.[1] Rather, the Quran was concerned that the Arabs had forgotten that God is the source of all wealth and increase in wealth. Both trading and raiding had become means of oppressing the weak and helpless in society. The *shari'a* enlarged upon the injunctions against illegitimate wealth in both the Quran and the traditions of the prophet to set down guidelines for almost all economic relationships.

---

1. Piracy was considered a legitimate approach to obtaining wealth by some Muslim governments right into the twentieth century. In abandoning piracy they were, however, not too many decades behind their European counterparts. A nominal or real state of war has always legitimated certain types of looting, with only the losers being required to return what they seize.

---

*Those who devour usury will not stand except as stand one whom the Satan by his touch Hath driven to madness. That is because they say: "Trade is like usury," but Allah hath permitted trade and forbidden usury.*
*(Quran 2:275)*

*Allah will deprive usury of all blessing, but will give increase for deeds of charity: For He loveth not any ungrateful and wicked.*
*(Quran 2:276)*

---

Under these guidelines a trustworthy worldwide system of trade relations developed, as well as local economic institutions which protected the rights of women and children and the right to private property, encouraged honesty, and allowed personal initiative. These diverse regulations did not amount to an economic theory, and certain legal fictions and devices were used to circumvent the letter of the *shari'a* when it inhibited trade. Yet the system overall helped make Islamic civilization at its height one of the wealthiest the world has known. It became an ideal of fairness, honesty, and recognition of God's sovereignty in economic relations.

Then in the nineteenth and twentieth centuries new economic theories, institutions, and legal standards were imposed on Muslim communities by the colonial powers. It is not surprising that in a time of rapid economic change there was a renewed interest in the *shari'a* provisions for economic relationships. This was especially so as the great majority of Muslims found themselves impoverished and economically marginalized in new capitalist economies. In answer to capitalism, and liberal economic theory generally, Muslim scholars have sought to articulate the economic principles upon which the *shari'a* regulations were built.

The basic principles of *shari'a* economics are that humans not presume on divine prerogatives, do not take what rightly belongs to those who are weaker, and do not enjoy an unfair profit. Buying or selling things that do not yet exist, such as the fruit anticipated from a blooming tree or the harvest anticipated from newly planted grain, presumes on God's sovereign control of the future and is forbidden. In some schools of law the same is true of selling things not actually in the possession of the seller.

Inheritance is strictly regulated so that no dependent or close relative is denied the share of an estate that God has ordained is his or hers. Provision is made for endowments of worthwhile institutions, but never to the exclusion of rightful heirs. *Shari'a* economics also forbids enjoying profit without sharing risk or taking unnecessary financial risks. Making loans at a fixed interest, which allows the lender an insured return on investment without sharing the risks of the borrower, is forbidden. Gambling, whether as a game or in risky trades and investments, is likewise forbidden. Contracts are strongly protected and must clearly state what is bought or sold and fix the price. However, in Islamic law oral rather than written contracts are regarded as valid, provided they are duly witnessed by competent, pious men.

These principles, and the laws which express them, rest uneasily with modern Western economic systems and ideas of economic justice. The *shari'a* assumes that money is a medium of exchange, not a commodity in itself. So the money market, which is so central to modern economic systems, is forbidden. The prohibition against lending at interest can sometimes be overcome through credit unions where a group shares the benefits and risks of loaning money to its members. More difficult in a world economy is insuring that every loan or investment supports activities in accordance with Islamic law and accumulating sufficient funds to finance large projects.

The kind of financing represented by stock and commodity markets is difficult or impossible since the sale of futures and options is forbidden. Scholars disagree over whether the *shari'a* protects non-tangible property, such as copyrights and patents on ideas and processes. And the same laws that insure that dependents and relatives receive an inheritance also insure that male relatives and children receive more than wives and female children. The legality of oral contracts places a high value on personal integrity, yet at the same time can make the auditing of accounts and tracing funds virtually impossible.

The development of Islamic economics, and associated institutions, has grown rapidly since the middle of the century. Courses and even degrees are available for students interested in this field, and the demand for Islamic financial services has been growing steadily. Yet in terms of even Muslim financial and trade activities they are small. The kinds of financial instruments forbidden by the *shari'a* exist because they were useful in fueling the enormous economic growth of the twentieth-century West. In the same way Muslim jurists 1,000 years ago developed legal fictions allowing the needs of commerce to overcome the letter of the law.

Yet if the *shari'a* regulations are to be developed into an *ideal* of divine economics, then such devices are clearly unacceptable. It remains an open question whether a purely Islamic economic system will lead to a vibrant international economy, or whether it will remain a marginal approach to finance for the pious. It is noteworthy that trade in the single most important commodity for Muslim economies, petroleum products, is sold in markets that operate completely at odds with the principles of Islamic law.

## The Shari'a as Family Law

The best-defined and most often followed part of the *shari'a* is that which deals with personal and family matters. The jurists were often overruled by political authorities, yet they were respected community leaders and the teachings they passed down from the Quran and *Sunnah*, as well as their own rulings, transformed family and private life. Islam radically transformed Arab society by reducing the status of blood ties to the immediate family except in connection with punishment of crimes (see above) and the duty of maintaining widows and orphans.

Ironically the freedom gained for individuals from the oppressive demands of clan and tribe puts the *shari'a* at odds with the intrusiveness of modern states into the personal and family affairs of their citizens. This is in part because the *shari'a* assumes inequalities in rights and power between men, women, and children that modern Western states have recently come to reject. It is partly because the responsibility for the welfare of all citizens that the *shari'a* assumes belongs to the family and local community has been assumed in the modern West by the state.

## Marriage and Divorce

Marriage according to the *shari'a* is primarily a contract between two responsible parties. The different schools of law disagree on the rights of a woman to refuse a marriage arranged by her father or male relatives, and whether she can enter into a marriage without their consent. The marriage contract is ended by divorce, which may be carried out by the husband with a simple declaration in front of witnesses, or may be sought by the wife by demonstrating appropriate grounds in a *shari'a* court. A marriage contract may specify conditions in which a divorce occurs automatically. Shiite law recognizes temporary marriage in which the contract is for a fixed period.

> *Abu Hurairah, may Allah be pleased with him, reported:*
> *"Allah's Messenger (may peace be upon him) said: 'A woman*
> *without a husband (or divorced or a widow) must not be married*
> *until she is consulted, and a virgin must not be married until her*
> *permission is sought.' They asked the Prophet of Allah (may peace*
> *be upon him) 'How her (virgin's) consent can be solicited?' He (the*
> *Holy Prophet) said: 'By keeping silent.'" (from Sahih Muslim)*

The marriage contract gives the husband far-ranging rights to restrict the activities of his wife and children, including the right to limit their movements to the home and to punish them physically. A woman has a right to refuse to travel with her husband and has control over her children until they reach age nine for boys and puberty for girls. After this age the husband, or his parents and male relatives, have right to custody and control of the children.

At marriage there is "bride gift," which in part pays for the woman's personal furnishing, and in part is held in trust to be returned to her in case of divorce. She has an absolute right to be maintained out of her husband's income, as do her children. She cannot be expelled from the household until it is conclusively proved that she doesn't bear her husband's child. Neither she nor her children can be denied their share of his estate by his adoption of other children or marriage to other wives.

Taken in sum the *shari'a* regulations of marriage greatly increased both the property and personal rights of women in Arab society. They were substantially in advance of the law found in most of Christendom at that time. In the context of a community where the friends and male relatives of a woman looked out for her welfare, and would take her in if she were divorced, they represented the most humane laws of the age. To many Muslims they remain an ideal of partnership in marriage and the protection of women's rights in divorce.

In most modern Western states, the *shari'a* ideal of marriage is problematic. The assumption that any man has rights over a woman has, in the twentieth century, been replaced with the idea that husband and wife are equal partners in marriage, with equal rights to communal property, children, and personal freedom. Moreover, in Western law it is usually assumed that the state, not the extended family, has ultimate responsibility for the welfare and support of its citizens.

In modern states laws protecting the privacy of the home do not extend to protecting the rights of either men or women to abuse one another, or their children, in the home. This said, it can hardly be argued that the modern Western family is an exemplar of stability and mutuality. Divorce rates are far higher in the West than in Islamic nations, and abuse of both children and spouses is found in all societies. Modern Muslims are divided on whether the *shari'a*, as traditionally interpreted, represents the answer to obvious problems and failings of the secular West, or whether it should be reinterpreted to give women and children the rights some believe are a logical extension of basic Quranic principles.

## The Shari'a and Gender Roles

Particularly with regard to family law, but in other realms as well, the *shari'a* as commonly interpreted gives men and women distinct and unequal social roles.[2] In addition to the differences in roles and rights in the family mentioned above, the *shari'a* specifies that women receive half as much inheritance as do their male siblings, and that their testimony in court cases has half the value of a man's.

---

*"The third important element in the Charter of Human Rights granted by Islam is that a woman's chastity must be respected and protected at all times"*

*Sayyid Abul A'la Mawdudi, in* Human Rights in Islam

*"Many Muslims, when they speak of human rights, either do not speak of women's rights at all or are mainly concerned with the question of how a woman's chastity may be protected."*

*Riffat Hassan, "On Human Rights and the Quranic Perspective," in* Human Rights in Religious Traditions

---

The actual role women play in different Muslim societies varies widely from this ideal. In some societies pre-Islamic cultural traditions of misogyny and patriarchy put women in positions shamefully less respected and

2. This does not necessarily distinguish it from Western law. It was only in the last decade of the twentieth century that Austria, my current residence, permitted women to work at night—aside from registered prostitutes.

empowered than is provided for according to the *shari'a*. One reason so many Muslim states would not recognize the Taliban in Afghanistan is that their treatment of women was sub-human, and thus sub-Islamic. Conversely in some Muslim societies in Southeast Asia the *shari'a* was interpreted in accordance with cultural traditions that stressed monogamy in marriage and gave women significant roles in both work and trade.

In some cases the pragmatic need to mobilize the strength of Muslim women in developing Muslim societies has led to new interpretations of exactly what the *shari'a* intends. And as Islam has spread among European and American men and women they likewise bring new viewpoints and attitudes to the interpretation of the *shari'a*. The confluence of these differing movements has led to the emergence of new and conflicting conceptualizations of the *shari'a* ideal for men and women, and significant women's movements in many traditional Muslim societies.

---

*But if we in the West look carefully at what is actually going on in the Middle East, if we can see behind the veil, it is clear that Muslim women are working hard to improve themselves and their families, to live comfortably and peaceably in the world. In that struggle, they are utilizing elements of their own tradition and culture. This includes Islam. For this, they are worthy of our admiration and respect. Their efforts offer alternate cultural methods to resolve the difference between males and females.*

*Elizabeth Warnock Fernea, from* Islamic Women Find a Different Voice

---

At the center of these movements is the issue of how the *shari'a* functions as the ideal for both men and women to realize their distinct, God-ordained roles. Most modernizing movements stress the general ideal that men and women are given different capabilities and can therefore ideally complement one another both in personal and social relationships. Some focus on maintaining egalitarianism in the face of "new" interpretations of Islam that limit women's options. Others stress the way that *shari'a* mandates clothing, as well as its general focus on the honor of women, can free them from being regarded as, or regarding themselves as, sex objects.

Some Western women who feel oppressed by the demands of being both mother and family provider profess to find in an apparently more limited role as mother and housewife a kind of freedom they did not have before. Moreover, a strictly defined role can provide security in the face of the overwhelming options seemingly provided by modern society. Other women maintain that the while the characters of men and women complement each other, they do not limit people to particular social roles. Amina Wadud and others have argued that the Quran, properly interpreted, is concerned with humanity as a whole. The *shari'a*, if discovered and interpreted without preconceived notions concerning sex roles, allows both men and women to have a wide range of roles based on their personal abilities and situation. What distinguishes all these approaches from modern feminism is the conviction that the *ideal* of personhood, and of womanhood, is found in God's will expressed in divine law.

## The Shari'a as a Guide to Ethics

The Islamic ideal, as understood by Ibn Tamiya, is submission to God's law, the *shari'a*. It is also a religion that promises that either an eternity in paradise, or in hell, will come to each person based on the sum of his or her good and evil deeds. Both the *jurists* and those who sought their guidance were interested in the relative weights of different types of sin, and the moral status of the minutest human actions.

## Sin and Punishment

In the orthodox view thoughts are not sins, or are the lightest of sins, unless they are put into action. They are not taken into account on the judgment day. One tradition of the Prophet states: "Allah does not take into account what the members of my community think, as long as they do not pronounce it or carry it out." *Dhanb*, mistakes or faults, are overcome by removing the fault that caused them through knowledge and good works. For the believer there was no need to seek special forgiveness for such mistakes.

Heavy sins, normally those involving the conscious breaking of God's commands, could be remedied through formally asking for forgiveness (*istighfar*), and through restitution if a person had been wronged. Such sins, although avoidable, were regarded as ubiquitous in humans and necessary so that humans would rely on God for mercy and forgiveness. A tradition states that Allah would eliminate his community if it didn't sin, and create another people who would commit sins, ask forgiveness, and be forgiven. Others, oft quoted, remind Muslims of the thousands of good works Allah makes available for them to compensate for their sins. It is said, for example, that each footstep toward the mosque wipes out a multitude of sins.

The ultimate sin, *shirk,* required repentance (*tawbah*), and the embracing of Islam through the confession of the one God, Allah, and the prophethood of Muhammad.

## The Five Grades of Moral Relevance

The jurists recognized in the Quran and Sunnah that not every deed could be classified simply as forbidden or allowed, and thus the books of law also classify human activities according to whether they are required (*fard*), encouraged (*mustahabb*), indifferent (*mubah*), discouraged (*makruh*), or prohibited (*haram*). In the day-to-day life of Muslims these distinctions are important as the basic moral guide. Most Muslims are strongly aware of which of these applies, and under what circumstances, to their daily actions.

---

*The Five Grades of Moral Relevance*

*Fard—required*

*Mustahabb—encouraged*

*Mubah—indifferent*

*Makruh—discouraged*

*Haram—prohibited*

---

For example, a number of different kinds of food are forbidden, including pork, alcoholic beverages, blood and blood products, bone marrow, and amphibious creatures. Conscientious Muslims will avoid these, and even food from kitchens where these were present. In the Muslim world there are also many alternative consumer goods to replace things like toothpaste, gelatin desserts, shampoo, and so on that are made with *haram* products. Muslims are also forbidden to expose certain parts of their bodies, and Muslim clothing is an important part of cultural and religious identity.

Having three grades of activities that were neither required nor forbidden, as well as the varying opinions of the four schools of law, makes the *shari'a* more flexible than many non-Muslims suppose. It also means that debate about ethical issues is not entirely circumscribed by the law. There have been conservative Muslim jurists who insisted that where no legal precedent existed no decision could be made. So for example a strict Hanbali jurist is said to have refrained from eating watermelons because he could not determine whether the seeds should be swallowed or spit out.

Not surprisingly some have gone as far as to deny that Muslims should participate in many aspects of modern life. Yet this viewpoint is clearly in the minority. In general, new situations have generated new *fatawa* (sing. *fatwa*) or legal rulings from recognized experts in the law. So, for example, when the first phonographs became available the question was raised as to whether recording the chanting of the Quran was permissible. Led by the head of Al-Azhar, the oldest and most famous Muslim university, a majority of jurists eventually agreed that it was.

More recently there has been debate over whether the use of tobacco was indifferent or discouraged. Some jurists have even ruled that its use is forbidden during fasting. Still, there are rulings that would surprise modern Westerners. Many conservative jurists believe that all musical performance (apart from reciting the Quran) is *haram* for Muslims: this despite the fact that almost all Muslim cultures have a strong musical tradition.

Having fixed designations for the moral desirability of each action or behavior will seem alien to many Christians. Yet in some respects the effort to discover what is wrong, necessary, and indifferent is no different than what individuals and ethicists do on a daily basis as they try to apply their faith to the ever-changing situations in which we live. On the other hand, the need to specify the moral category into which every possible action belongs reflects the Muslim *ideal* that divine law should regulate all of life. Ethics in the end is submission to that law rather than the exercise of well-intentioned free will.

## The Final Judgment

In the end the jurists understood that sin is punishable by God, who sees and knows all things. Muslim belief includes a detailed account of what all humans can expect both when they are in the grave, and at the final judgment. In the grave Muslims will find rest and peace, while two angels will ceaselessly torture non-Muslims. At the final judgment the deeds, good and evil, of each person will be weighed in a balance. Those whose good deeds outweigh their evil deeds will pass easily over a bridge into paradise. Those whose evil deeds are heavier will try to cross the bridge but will find that it has narrowed to the width of a knife blade, and will fall off into hell. There they may still hope for rescue, as each of the true prophets (including Moses, Jesus, and Muhammad) will gather his followers after they have suffered for some time and bring them to paradise. *Muslims are quick to point out that deeds, rather than beliefs, determine one's eternal fate.* The *shari'a* has the final word on human life, but for Muslims it is a way of mercy, not judgment.

## The Shari'a and the Future of Muslim Societies

In the twentieth century deep conflicts have emerged between the *shari'a* ideal for society and the prevailing norms for modern states. The difficulty this poses for Muslims is compounded by the situation in which even the vestiges of classical Islamic civilization have crumbled, leaving most Muslims living in modern states, sometimes as majorities and sometimes as minorities, but rarely under an Islamic government of any sort.

Just as Muslim leaders and intellectuals have tried in various ways to reexamine and appropriate the precedents of Islam's golden age under the rightly guided caliphs, so they have analyzed and reevaluated the nature of *shari'a* in order to give divine law its appropriate place in Muslim society. Leaving aside Muslims who essentially subordinate the *shari'a* to other political ideologies, there are still several approaches to finding the appropriate role of the *shari'a* in Muslim society.

The most conservative traditionalists have taken the position that the *shari'a* is identical with the classical books of law (or some subset of which they approve) and that an authentically Muslim society will simply conform itself to these. The most notable experiment of this kind was made in Afghanistan under the Taliban. Their efforts to enforce the minutest details of their version of Islamic law are well known, and the cost is well documented. Although similar movements in other countries are less likely to obtain power, they often play an important political role.

In most countries with a Muslim majority a promise to Islamicize the laws and society has political benefits. If for some minority this means exactly implementing the classical books of law, then insecure governments looking for support will find ways to cater to that minority. In Pakistan different aspects of the *shari'a* have thus been implemented over the last two decades, including the Quranic punishments for certain crimes (mentioned above) as well as a law requiring the death penalty for blasphemy. In countries like Malaysia and Indonesia there have been intense political struggles over the implementation of the *shari'a*, and pressure to implement at least parts of it to satisfy a vocal and politically active minority.

In these same countries, and many others, both government officials and intellectuals are actively discussing other approaches to the *shari'a*. While there are continual debates about specific issues, there is increasing agreement that the *shari'a* is not just a fixed tradition of laws, but a living legal tradition in which *ijithad* plays a role.

A more conservative approach looks to the al-Shafi'is fours roots of the *shari'a* as a basis for developing new rulings on particular social and political issues, with the understanding that *consensus* does not mean the consensus of the four schools of law, but of modern scholars faced with similar situations. Others maintain that modern governments need to return to the guidelines of the earliest jurists, which included the overall good of the community, the use of personal judgment in unique cases, and the implementation of local cultural rules when consistent with the Quran and Sunnah. Finally, there are those who, without denying the utility of the books of law or the precedents of the classical jurists, believe the *shari'a* needs to be reconceived as a *methodology* for realizing Islam in each age and situation.

Rethinking the *shari'a* in terms of methodology is an approach that fits well with the broad goal of the Islamization of knowledge suggested by Fazlur Rahman and can be seen as part of an overall intellectual project to rebuild Islamic civilization from the ground up. Yet this kind of approach faces stiff political competition from groups like the Muslim Brotherhood, Hamas, and the Hezbollah. These radical groups have founded flexible political, social, and military organizations implementing their Islamic vision on a realistic, ad hoc basis without waiting to form a consistent intellectual vision.

Among the most impoverished and marginalized Muslims such groups seem to offer more promising, or at least immediate, solutions than those of either intellectuals or the traditional *ulama*. The future shape and role of the *shari'a* in Muslim life may well depend on which group can produce the concrete improvements in daily life that will raise the majority of Muslims out of abject poverty and powerlessness. For far too many Muslims Qutb's accusation that their great civilization has sunk back into the pre-Islamic situation of *jahilia* under corrupt and dictatorial leaders is both an observable truth and a political imperative.

## Conclusion

When Muhammad received the Quran and shared it with his friends and relatives, they were transformed by its vision of humanity and human society. The Oneness of God was mirrored in the oneness of humanity, and God's demand for equality and justice among humans was underscored by the promise of God's judgment upon all, regardless of rank or religion, who violated that justice. The *shari'a*, however it might be enforced or ignored in the vicissitudes of human history, has been a potent symbol of human equality and dignity under revealed law. It bound ruler and peasant alike. Mastery belonged to anyone with the piety and resoluteness to master its sources and apply common human reason to them. Yet it was master over all.

In this respect it is different from legislation arising out of political processes, which even in the best of democracies sometimes excuses the lawmaker from the provisions of the law, and favors the interests of the rich and powerful over the weak. In the West the ideal of democracy and the final triumph of an informed electorate animates faith in the law against the reality of its shortcomings. Most Muslims have no experiential basis for sharing this faith. They do know that if they follow the path of *shari'a*, whatever the failings of their rulers, it will lead them to justice, and finally to God, just as those who refuse to follow it will find their way leads to judgment, and finally oblivion.

## Guide for Further Study

Review the key themes of the chapter. If members of the study group have questions about the these key themes it would be good to discuss these first.

### Key Themes

- For Muslims obedience to God's law is the essence of religion.
- The fundamental sources of the *shari'a* (divine law) are the Quran, the Sunnah, and the consensus of experts over how the clear regulations in these can be extended by analogy.

- Over several centuries there developed a vast body of Islamic law regulating virtually every part of Muslim society.

- This law covered religious belief and practice, human relationships of all sorts, and government.

- The *shari'a* is also a guide to Muslim ethics. It tells Muslims whether any action or relationship is forbidden or allowed, and how they can do good, avoid sin, and make up for their failings so that they do not fall under God's judgment.

- The classical books of law have some regulations that are at odds with the principles of modern, non-Muslim democracies.

- Modern Muslim reform movements have varying ideas about how divine law should be implemented in modern society. Some wish to impose exactly the classical system of law. Others wish to use this system as a guide to how divine law is developed. Others wish to return to more fundamental principles found in the first generation of Muslims.

## Final Questions for Discussion

- As followers of a religion that emphasizes obedience to God's law, modern Muslims are intensely interested in defining that law in modern situations. Often they turn to Muslim legal scholars for an interpretation of Islamic law. How is this similar to, and different from, Christian approaches to applying the principles of the Bible to modern issues?

- Muslims in the United States and Europe are seeking to both understand their role as religious people in secular societies, and to make a contribution to the development of their religion overall. What are some of the challenges facing Christians in societies where Muslims are a growing and increasingly visible minority?

- How are Christian demands that governments uphold God's law different from those of Muslims demanding the implementation of the *shari'a*?

- The *shari'a* makes provision for religious minorities in a dominantly Muslim state. How is its approach different from that of your nation or community?

- How do you think God wishes relations between men and women to be regulated?

- How is the economic theory of modern capitalist nations different from that of the *sharia*?

- The *sharia* specifies exactly how Muslims should worship. What regulates the patterns of Christian worship?

## Additional Readings

In the readings below, we find two Muslims reflecting on how *sharia* can and should play a role in modern societies. Rahman is primarily interested in building a new Muslim society based on *sharia;* one which will overcome and improve on a morally impoverished secular society. Ramadan is concerned with the problem of if Muslim can remain faithful to divine law while living as a religious minority in secular Europe.

Rahman, Fazlur. *Islam and Modernity.* Chicago: University of Chicago Press, 1982.

### Excerpts from Chapter 4

1. Islamic theology is certainly an intellectual endeavor, but it is so in the sense that it gives a coherent and faithful account of what is there in the Quran so that a believing person or a person prone to believe can give consent both from the mind and from the heart and make this world view his or her mental and spiritual home. . . . AlGhazali had long ago condemned the official "science of theology" because it was neither spiritually satisfying nor intellectually satisfactory—he called it the game of intellectual children! Yet this seems to be the fate of most historical theologies . . .

A God that speaks neither to the intellect of man nor to his heart, nor yet can generate a system of values for man, is considerably worse than nothing and is better off dead.

The question of who should interpret law has been acute in Islamic societies because of the historical accident that the so-called law (*fiqh*) has been the result of the work of private lawyers, while in the later medieval centuries governments—particularly the Ottoman government—had to promulgate laws on issues not covered by the *Sharia* law . . .

The only way to produce genuine Islamic law is to enlighten public conscience, particularly that of the educated classes, with Islamic values. This, in fact, underlines the necessity of working out Islamic ethics systematically from the Quran and making such works accessible to the general reader. There is no shortcut to this process for the production of Islamic law . . . If firstrate works on the history of Islamic law and jurisprudence are written—as I have argued must be done—these should be made required reading in the schools of law as part of the normal curriculum. In this way, key Islamic legal and moral concepts would gradually come to inform the legal profession

As a system of values, Islam naturally cannot favor a laissez-faire society. On the other hand, Islam knows well that coercion does not pay or even work. As for indoctrination in the sense of brainwashing, I have already pointed out that this technique of creating future generations of the faithful in fact ultimately backfires. (pp. 156–57, 159)

## Additional Questions

- Rahman wants to enlighten the public regarding Islamic values as a basis for creating Islamic laws. How do you think religious values should influence the creation of laws?

- Do you think Islamic values should play a role in shaping laws in a society that also has non-Muslims?

- Do you think Christian values play a role in shaping laws in a society with non-Christians?

Ramadan, Tariq. *To Be a European Muslim.* Leicester, UK: The Islamic Foundation, 1999.

## Excerpts from Part III (on Muslims living their faith in the European context and legal ramifications)

1. The Islamic teachings grafted on faith in the Oneness of God (*tawhīd*) are based on the "principle of justice" which, in every circumstance, for or against Muslims, has to be applied first. The life of the heart, emotion or affection, even though they are of great importance in Islam must be directed and mastered by rules which allow people to live together.

We saw when discussing the notion of belonging in Islam that it is a very important element within Muslim life, but that still it should by no means warrant injustice or betrayal. Muslims are bound by faith, conscience and justice and nothing can justify an exception to this rule, be it towards a Muslim or not. . . . In other words, while some scholars wanted, in terms of allegiance, to set the reference to the Islamic way (*Shari'a*) against that of a country's constitution, we now realize that it is in the name of the teachings of *Shari'a* that Muslims must respect the legal framework of the country they live in. . . .

As residents and citizens, living in peace and security, Muslims have to provide themselves with all the means that will enable them to protect their identity and, at the same time, to bear witness to the Message of Islam before their native fellow citizens. This twofold dimension of *shahada alIslam* cannot be realized by living in isolation, far from the surrounding society, curled up inside the Muslim community. It is exactly the contrary that turns out to be required: to be a Muslim in Europe means to interact with the whole of society at different levels (from local up to national and even continental involvement). . . .

This is what Muslims have to ask themselves and of the society they live in. As they are surrounded by all this high technology, swept along by the current of progress, there nevertheless arises a question, stemming from their hearts, in the name of their identity: What about God? What about spirituality? What is the meaning of all this effervescence, agitation and turmoil we witness in our modern life? (pp. 213–16)

## Conclusion

. . .With varying rhythms, according to the modalities proper to each country, the outline of a European Muslim identity is in the course of being drawn . . . European social players and intellectuals are increasingly feeling this and are already engaged in constructive dialogue and engagement in the field with their Muslim partners. . . . it is the responsibility of the people of Faith and conscience to try to defend and live up to their principles regardless of the results obtained, even if it seems that the whole world is against them. This because they know the price of faithfulness to God and to their own conscience. (pp. 233–35)

Additional Questions

- Although Muslims are a minority in Europe, Ramadan believes they must play a role in both preserving their identity and shaping society. In what matters should religious minorities give in to the majority?
- In what matters must they take a stand and refuse to compromise?

### Selections from *Sahih Muslim*

The following excerpts from various types of Muslim law will give some insight into what the *shari'a* actually consists of. Muslims often speak of *shari'a* as if it were a well-defined body of law. In fact the term *shari'a* refers to a wide range of legal works in a variety of forms, as can be seen below. These are found the *Sahih Muslim* as produced by the National Muslim Student Association of the USA and Canada (http://www.usc.edu/dept/MSA/). These selections are only a fragment of the entire work, which has much more detail about possible variations on the crime.

*Chapter 1: Punishment for theft and the minimum limit according to which it is imposed upon an offender.*

*Book 17, Number 4175:*

> 'A'isha reported that Allah's Messenger (may peace be upon him) cut off the hand of a thief for a quarter of a dinar rid upwards.

*Book 17, Number 4180:*

> A Hadith like this has been narrated on the authority of Yazid b. 'Abdullah b. al-Had with the same chain of transmitters.

*Book 17, Number 4181:*

> 'A'isha reported that during the lifetime of Allah's Messenger (may peace be upon him) the hand of the thief was not cut off for less than the price of a shield, iron coat or armor and both of them are valuable.

*Chapter 3: Prescribed punishment for an adulterer and an adulteress.*

*Book 17, Number 4191:*

> 'Ubada b. as-Samit reported: Allah's Messenger (may peace be upon him) as saying: Receive (teaching) from me, receive

(teaching) from me. Allah has ordained a way for those (women). When an unmarried male commits adultery with an unmarried female (they should receive) one hundred lashes and banishment for one year. And in case of married male committing adultery with a married female, they shall receive one hundred lashes and be stoned to death.

*(The following Hadith describes the punishment of apostasy. Muslim jurists regarded apostasy as a form of treason. Some modern commentators regard this as the reason that apostasy is justifiably punished by death. It is not seen as a matter of religious belief, but of betraying the community.)*

*Book 38, Number 4339:*

Narrated Aisha, Ummul Mu'minin:

The Apostle of Allah (peace be upon him) said: The blood of a Muslim man who testifies that there is no god but Allah and that Muhammad is Allah's Apostle should not lawfully be shed except only for one of three reasons: a man who committed fornication after marriage, in which case he should be stoned; one who goes forth to fight with Allah and His Apostle, in which case he should be killed or crucified or exiled from the land; or one who commits murder for which he is killed.

## Ayatullah Al Uzama Syed Abul Qasim El Khoei. *Taudhihul Masae'l* (Islamic Laws). Islamic Seminary Publications. Found at http://al-islam1.org/laws/al-khui/.

*These laws are from a well-known contemporary Shiite jurist. They are not greatly different from the kind of rules found among other Sunni jurists. The reader can see that rather than quoting various Hadith, the author simply reiterates directly the rules found in his school of law. As in the previous sections, these are only small excerpts of much lengthier sections. The rules on prescribed time for midday and afternoon prayers run to several pages.*

*Prescribed time for midday and afternoon prayers.*

737. If a stick or anything similar to it, which is called indicator (*shakhis*) is inserted in a leveled ground its shadow will fall towards west when the sun rises in the morning and as the sun continues to rise the shadow of the indicator decreases. And in

our cities it becomes smallest at the time of the commencement of midday. And when midday passes the shadow of the indicator turns towards east and as the sun moves towards west the shadow goes on increasing. Hence when the shadow reaches the last stage of shortness and begins increasing again it is known that midday has taken place. However, in some cities e.g. in Mecca the shadow becomes extinct sometimes and when it reappears it becomes known that it is midday.

738. The time prescribed for midday and afternoon prayers is from the declining of the sun till sunset. However, if a person intentionally offers afternoon prayers earlier than midday prayers his prayer is void except when sufficient time is not left for more than one prayers. In that event if a person has not offered midday prayers it becomes *qaza* and he should offer afternoon prayers. And if before that time a person offers complete afternoon prayers before midday prayers by mistake his prayers is valid. And it is better that he should treat that prayers to the midday prayers and should offer 4 more units of prayers with the intention of nearness to Allah (*Mafis zima Qurbatan ilial lah*).

*Divorce*

2507. The man who divorces his wife must be adult and sane and should divorce her of his own free will. Hence, it he is forced to divorce her, the divorce will be void. It is also necessary that the man has an intention of divorcing her. If, therefore, he pronounces the formula of divorce only in jest, the divorce is not valid.

2508. It is necessary that when a woman is divorced she should be free from menses and lochia. It is also necessary that her husband should not have had sexual intercourse with her during the period of her purity. The details of these two conditions will be given in the succeeding Articles.

2509. It is valid to divorce a woman even if she is in menses and lochia in the following three circumstances:

i. The husband has not had sexual intercourse with her after marriage.

ii. It may be known that she is pregnant. In case, however, this fact is not known and the husband divorces her during menses, and comes to know later that she was pregnant, the obligatory precaution is that he should divorce her again.

iii. On account of the husband's being absent or under imprisonment, he may not be able to ascertain whether or not she is
pure of menses or lochia.

## Khums (or Zakat the obligatory tithe or tax paid by all Muslims)

1760. It is obligatory to pay Khums on the following seven things:

(i) Profit or gain from earning. (ii) Minerals (iii) Treasure-trove.
(iv) Mingling of lawful property with unlawful property. (v) Gems
obtained from the sea: by diving. (vi) War booty. (vii) Land which
a zimmi (an infidel living under the protection of Islamic Government) purchases from a Muslim.

1761. If a person earns something by means of trade, industry or
any other profession (for example, if he earns some money by offering prayers and fasting on behalf of a dead person) and this
earning of his exceeds his own annual expenses as well those of
his family he should pay Khums (i.e. 1/5) of the property in accordance with the relevant orders, which will be mentioned later.

1762. If a person comes across some property without having to
work for it (for example, if someone gives him something as a
gift,) and that property exceeds his own annual expenses as well as
those of his family he should pay Khums of the property.

1763. It is not obligatory to pay Khums of the dowry (Mehr) which
a woman gets, or on the property, which a husband gets in lieu of
divorcing his wife by way of khula: and the same rule applies to the
property, which one inherits. If some property is inherited from
whom no inheritance was expected, the obligatory precaution is
that in case the property so inherited is in excess of the annual
expenses of oneself and one's family, one should pay Khums of the
excess property.

## Unlawful transactions

2063. The following six kinds of transactions are unlawful:

i. To sale and purchase basically impure (najis) things, e.g.
intoxicating beverages, non-hunting dogs, a dead body or a
pig. As regards other impure things, their sale and purchase
is permissible only if it is proposed to obtain lawful gain from
them (e.g. manufacturing manure from faeces), although, as
a precaution, their sale and purchase should also be avoided.

ii. Sale and purchase of usurped property.

iii. On the basis of precaution sale and purchase of those things which are not usually considered to be merchandise is unlawful (for example, the sale and purchase of ferocious beasts).

iv. Any transaction which involves interest.

v. Sale and purchase of those things which are usually utilized for an unlawful act only (e.g. gambling tools).

vi. To sell a thing in which something else is mixed and it is neither possible to detect the adulteration nor the seller informs the buyer about it (e.g. to sell ghee mixed with fat). This act is called cheating (*ghash*) or adulteration. The holy Prophet of Islam has said: "If a person sells something to the Muslims or harms them, or practices deceit upon them, he is not one of my followers. And as and when a person cheats his brother Muslim (i.e. sells him an adulterated commodity) Allah deprives him of his livelihood, closes the means of his earnings and leaves him to himself (i.e. deprives him of His blessings).

Ayatullah al-'Uzma al-Sayyid 'Ali al-Husayni al-Seestani. *Contemporary Legal Rulings in Shī'ite Law.* Stanmore, UK: World Federation of KSI Muslim Communities, n. d. Found at http://al-islam1.org/laws/.

*The following rulings in Islamic law were made by a respected Shiite judge in response to questions from ordinary Muslims. It is a common practice for prominent Muslim jurists to issue such rulings (fatawa), and for them to be published in newspapers, magazines, and on the Internet. While some jurists and institutions have more prestige or political power than others, there is no central authority in Islam to determine which rulings are valid are invalid. The selections below demonstrate how important ritual purity remains for Muslims.*

### Ritual Purity (taharah)

Q1: It often happens that I shake hands with someone while my hands are wet. I do not know whether the one with whom I shook hands is a Muslim or an unbeliever (*kāfir*), who is not regarded as ritually pure (*tathir*). Is it obligatory for me to ask him in order to make sure?

A: Certainly not. It is not obligatory for you to ask him. You may say the hand with which I touched his hand was ritually pure. (FM, pp. 398–99)

Q2: A university student, businessman, tourist or some such person travels to a non-Muslim country, say, Europe, such that scarcely a day passes without direct contact with its Christian and Jewish inhabitants, with the attendant moisture exchange in the cafe, or at the barber shop, doctor's office, dry cleaner's, etc. making it difficult to count (the places). What should he do?

A: He should assume the ritual purity of their bodies as long as he does not know that their ritual impurity (*najasah*) was acquired from an external source. (FM, p. 399)

Q4: An electrically-operated washing machine can dry clothes, after the water supply is cut off from it, due to the power of spinning rather than squeezing. Is that enough for their ritual purification (*tathir*)?

A: Yes, that is enough for their ritual purification. (FM, p. 398)

Q5: Some people throw newspapers, magazines and some respected books in the garbage, although they contain some verses of the Quran or names of Allah (s.w.t.).

A: This is not permissible and it is obligatory to take them out of such places and to purify them if they have come into contact with some ritual impurity. (FM, p. 419)

## Additional Questions

The form of law found above differs from the legal codes of most nations.

- How is the basis of Islamic law different from the laws of your country?
- How are the concerns of Islamic law different from the laws in your country?
- If religious ritual and purity are required by God, why should not the government enforce these laws?
- What makes the laws on prayer time and ritual purity different from those on theft or adultery?

## Another Muslim Look at Law

The two poems below represent a commentary on those who misuse the distinction between belief and dis-belief. As you read them ask yourself whether your deepest beliefs differ from the dogma taught in Christian churches.

Rabi'a. "I carry a torch in one hand." from *Doorkeeper of the heart: versions of Rabia*, translated by Charles Upton. Putney, VT: Threshold, 1988.

> I carry a torch in one hand
> And a bucket of water in the other:
> With these things I am going to set fire to Heaven
> And put out the flames of Hell
> So that voyagers to God can rip the veils
> And see the real goal.

Kahf, Mohja. "'The Water of Hajar' and Other Poems." In *Muslim World*, edited by Jane I. Smith and Ibrahim Abu Rabi', Vol. 91, 2001.

Compassion

*Preface: In January 1998 gunmen massacred 120 men, women and children moviegoers in a cinema during Algeria's civil conflict.*

> By the hunger of the children of Iraq
> By the sound of frantic running in Kosovo
> By the swollen bodies in a river in Rwanda
> and Afghani women and the writers of Algiers,
> I am a disbeliever
>
> in everything that refuses to kiss full on the lips
> the ones still living
> and receive them in the bosom of the self,
> no matter the religion or the nation or the race
> I am a disbeliever in everything
> that does not say "How was the movie? I love you"
>
> I need a body outside my life to travel and kneel
> on the sidewalk beside a movie theater in Algiers

over the bodies of the supple children
who will never be my children's playmates or marry them
over the bodies of the men and women
will never phone me or you from Algiers
"How was the movie? I love you. I love you.

I need time outside the world
where I can whisper in the ear of every one,
By God, by God, you will never be forgotten
By God, I will make sure the world
buries its face in your beautiful hair,
sings to you, learns your name and your music,
lifts you up in the crook of its arm like a gift

I am a disbeliever
in everything but the purity of the bodies
of the men and women with or without the veil,
in everything but the suppleness of the children
I am a disbeliever in every scripture that leaves out
"How was the movie? I love you. I love you."

# Epilogue—The Shaking of the Foundations

Since the beginning of the twenty-first century the faith and values of the great majority of Muslims worldwide have been overshadowed by the violent actions of a small number of Muslim terrorists. For Christians living in the West the effects of these terrorist groups have been sporadic. For many Muslims in the majority-Muslim nations they have become the continually erupting background of daily life. In some Muslim nations, notably Syria and Afghanistan, they are the foreground that dominates every decision and every possibility. As a result, for many Muslims it is a struggle to look beyond survival to the aspiration of being a witness to and creator of a civilization reflecting God's beneficence.

The reasons for the current situation in the majority-Muslim world are well known. Colonialism destroyed the longstanding social structures that gave the Muslim world stability. More recently the US and coalition military engagements in Iraq and Afghanistan that were intended to put a stop to the terrorist threat realized on 9/11/2001 set ablaze sectarian rivalries that had long smoldered in these and other Muslim lands. The Arab Spring in 2010 tore off the thin veneer of governance that hid the suppressed anarchy beneath Muslim societies from Libya to Syria.

Iran's ambitious expansion of its regional influence, and responses to it from wealthy Sunni states in the Arabian Peninsula continually increase the availability of arms for a wide variety of terrorist and insurgent groups. And from West Africa, across the Horn of Africa to Pakistan, the incapacity and even unwillingness of national governments to combat such groups has put both Muslims and non-Muslims at constant risk of violence. The resulting anarchy has created safe spaces for terrorist groups to take refuge, train, and prepare for fresh attacks.

Even as these headline-grabbing events have shaped worldwide perceptions of Islam and Muslims, the movement of Islam to areas outside the traditional Muslim world has become more apparent. While Muslims remain small minorities in the West they have become the object of great attention and often suspicion. The suspicion makes living as a modern Western Muslim difficult. But the attention offers fresh opportunities to express Muslim values and faith. And majority-Muslim populations in Malaysia and Indonesia, spared the political turmoil and violence of their brothers and sisters, find that with Muslims in the West they have the opportunity to shape Islam from its geographic margins.

These changes highlight the fact that Islam has always been, like Christianity, a transnational religion. In the midst of globalization the Muslim reality has become determined by both global and local culture. Transnational militant movements such as al-Qaeda and ISIS may try to create a "cyber-caliphate" worldwide, but to survive they have sought to put their imprint on the political structures of dominantly Muslim nations and must thus be supported or resisted locally. Muslims who simply wish to live at peace in whichever social and cultural environment they find themselves are drawn into the international arena.

But transnational Islam isn't always militant. It also includes groups like the Muslim World Federation and its efforts to spread Wahhabi-inspired Islamic ideologies worldwide, the Hizmat Movement associated with Fetullah Gulen and its worldwide secular science-oriented school systems, and even individual teachers like Tarik Ramadan who travel worldwide promoting the idea that Islam is compatible with secular democracy.

There is no single Islamic political world, despite the pretensions of the terrorists. The Hadhra party of Tunisia is different from the Muslim Brotherhood that was recently ousted from government by Egypt's military. And both are different from the Justice and Development Party in Turkey, or the People's Justice Party in Malaysia. None is remotely similar to the Taliban that continues to seek a return to power in Afghanistan, and none (including the Taliban) represents the political aspirations of Muslims living in the West.

The most important question, however, is whether there exists a global world of shared Muslim faith and values, and how it might be changing. For it is Muslims' values that will underlie emergent political and social systems in dominantly Muslim lands and will determine how Muslim minorities shape their lives outside the Islamic world.

Muslims, and indeed all peoples, respond to the challenges of their situation within what Charles Taylor calls a "social imaginary," the range of possible social structures that the members of a society can imagine.[1] Even

1. Taylor, *Modern Social Imaginaries,* 23–24.

in the Christian West the social imaginary of different societies (England and France, for example) were strikingly different in the eighteenth and nineteenth centuries and remain different today. The development of modern democratic societies thus took place in different ways, at different rates, and remain characterized by different institutional forms and different ways in which the citizens of these countries relate to those institutions.

The Muslim world is not only as varied as Europe, but the social imaginaries found within it vary considerably from those present in the modern West. And the place where they vary most is in the concept of personal choice in relation to religiously motivated participation in public life.

Charles Taylor points out that the "public sphere" in the modern Western social imaginary is the place where a vast variety of different opinions and viewpoints engage in discussion of social issues. The Western social imaginary that emerges from this discussion values the most rational and representative choices for the society as a whole. And these are regarded as legitimate precisely because of the mechanism (public discourse) out of which they arose. Such ideas are not far from those advanced by Rached Ghanoushi in Tunisia, Tariq Ramadan in Europe and the United States, and Fetullah Gulen in Turkey. They are in sharp contrast to the social imaginary of those Muslims, both militant and non-militant, for whom only the re-iteration of the Islam imagined to have existed at the time of the Prophet Muhammad can be legitimately Muslim.

For the current social imaginary of the West to have arisen in the West at least three socially shared convictions needed to emerge. The first was that the deepest and most important religious convictions are both a privilege and a burden belonging to the individual alone. Religious convictions need not be expressed in the ordering of society for the individual to be fully his or her religious self. Secondly the will of God for human societies must be understood to be fully public, observable by any reasonable person regardless of religious convictions. And third and following from this, no religious community should have a monopoly on the relationship of religious truth to public life. The public sphere should possess a variety of religious opinions including the option of no religion, and no one of them should monopolize public decision-making.

Despite the leadership of intellectuals like Ghanousi, Ramadan, and others, this social imaginary does not yet exist in most of the dominantly Muslim world, just as it didn't exist in the pre-modern Christian West and does not exist in much of the world outside the north Atlantic nations. The majority of Muslims do not yet imagine that either being Muslim or being a member of a particular Muslim sect is a matter of personal choice with primarily individual consequences. One's sectarian affinity is part of one's primal identity, an identity into which one is born and from which one cannot escape. It binds one fundamentally and irrevocably to others and is the primary source of one's social identity.

Nor does it appear that most Muslims imagine that God's will is adequately known for the purpose of ordering society without reference to the revelation that is particular to and definitive of their religion.

Nor does it appear that most Muslims imagine a social world organized on the basis of a public discussion that regards all religious views as possessing an equal right to participate. For most Muslims it is self-evident that Islam, or their version of Islam, should have a privileged place in the public sphere, since it is the sole complete representation of the will of God.

Understanding this will help us better understand groups like the Muslim Brotherhood, or al-Qaeda or Hezbollah or even Turkey's Justice and Development Party. These parties are not problematic because they represent particular policies and behaviors that their rivals or victims dislike. That is true of all modern political parties and movements. *The problem from with each of these from the standpoint of both the modern West and contemporary Christian thought is that it doesn't imagine itself as one among many choices for Muslims and non-Muslims.*

It imagines itself as the sole truly Islamic choice, and indeed the sole legitimate ordering power in human society. Put another way, it appears that these groups can only imagine a single-party Muslim state. That each of these may be forced temporarily to "share power," whether with other Muslim parties or with non-religious political parties, is simply a pragmatic arrangement, not a commitment to pluralist democracy in which all voices always have equal access to the public square.

*Yet this may be changing and changing rapidly.* Even as I write this epilogue in 2018, Muslims in Egypt, Turkey, and Iran have taken to the streets against Islamist governments. What makes these protests different is that they are not part of the previous politics of the street where rival political movements call their followers out in a show of force to represent the movement's interests. Instead they represent a generalized public refusal to accept the autocracy and paternalism that are at the core of the old Islamist political imagination.

They represent the assertion that democracy is not merely the public ratification of the right of a particular person or party to rule on God's behalf (which is the way classical Islam understood the public role in government). They are asserting that they, the people, possess the right to rule. Government doesn't govern in God's name with their assent. It governs in *their name* with their assent and represents neither its own interests nor those it purports God to have.

If I am right then what is happening on the street in the Muslim world is the real beginning of democracy in the Muslim world, because it reaches beneath democratic forms to a truly democratic social imagination. It suggests the emergence of new ways of valuing humanity in its relationship to God and God's will.

At the same time anyone with an interest in democracy should be cautious. Only part of the democratic imagination involves "people's power." The other part imagines that all people possess it equally. The Marrakesh Declaration of 2016 (found the Appendix) notwithstanding, it remains to be seen whether contemporary Muslims understand that at least in the public realm all religious opinions should be equal.

Yet we do find among many Muslims, and even broadly in some Muslim societies, a recognition that a religiously plural society cannot be governed effectively if one particular religion or sect has a monopoly in public discourse. Tunisia, Malaysia, and Indonesia are laboratories where the chemistry of this modern idea in political life is being vigorously, even explosively, explored. Popular Muslim writers and speakers have forcefully asserted the need for a modern Muslim understanding of the relationship of religion to public discourse and the ordering of modern societies. It remains to be seen whether Muslims will find that equally valuing all voices is a distinctly Muslim value, based in a distinctly Islamic faith.

---

The circle of people whose religion has the *shahadah* at its center is vast. If Islam is just defined in terms of those who acknowledge Allah as the one God and Muhammad as his Prophet, then it may well be the fastest growing religion in the world. The circle of those who actually live out the five pillars of Islam, or even hold them as an ideal, is smaller. There are those calling themselves Sufi Muslims who believe their rituals and spirituality transcend the mundane interpretation of the pillars. There are Black Muslims whose faith was defined more by Elijah Muhammad than classical Sunni Islam. There are Sikhs, Bahais, and sectarian Muslim groups whose religion springs from Islam but no longer makes the pillars central to it. Smaller still is the circle of those who understand and assent to all the beliefs in the classical creeds. Even within that circle there are differences. Shiites and Sunni Muslims are distinct, and in both the Shi' and Sunni communities are others with distinctive legal practices and beliefs.

Running through almost all Muslim communities are beliefs, prejudices, and the remnants of pre-Islamic worldviews that scholars call "folk" Islam. If the Islamic faith is submission of the human heart to God then one could argue there are as many types of Islam as there are believers. Yet Muslims will say that there is only one Islam. It is the way of the one God, revealed through the last Prophet, with the final revelation, for all of humanity. Beyond the many ideals we encounter among Muslims, some of which we may resonate with and others of which we may question, *tawhid* will be the center of faith, and Allah its object and consummation.

# Suggestions for Further Exploration

- Arrange a visit to a local mosque to observe a worship service or time of prayer. Make sure you let the imam (head of the mosque) know in advance that you are coming.

- Invite an imam to speak to your group and answer questions.

- Visit a local Muslim school and learn about how it is similar to, and different from, Christian schools.

- Invite a Muslim who has made the pilgrimage to Mecca to come and share their experience with your group.

- Invite Muslim women to speak to your group about their religious experience and how Islam affects their understanding of their role in the family and society.

# Glossary

*'adhāb al-kabr*, suffering in the grave by those who have sinned.

*Allah^u akbar*, "God is the greatest."

*āyah* (pl. *āyāt*), Sentence or sign. Among the signs of God are the created order. The verses of the Quran are also *āyāt*.

*Ayatollah*, the highest ranking scholar of law in Twelver Shī'ite religious hierarchy

*barakah*, blessing, or divine power emanating from a holy man.

*bay'ah*, contract of oath of allegiance to the Caliph.

*bid'a*, innovation.

*dār al-Harb*, realm of war, territory not under Islamic law and therefore subject to conquest by Muslims.

*dār al-Islam*, realm of peace, territory under Islamic rule.

*dār al-Sul*, realm of treaty, regions which in the early years of Islam were protected from Muslim aggression by treaty.

*dervish, darwish*, Turkish and Persian respectively for *sufi*.

*dhanb*, light sins, mistakes.

*dhikr*, remembrance of God.

*dhimmī, alh al-dhimma*, Jews, Christians and other accepted by treaty as subjects under Muslim rule and entitled to legal protection in return for payment of taxes and certain restrictions on their public religious activities.

*dīn*, religion, religions as a way of life.

*fanā'*, extinction of self preceding the experience of unity with God.

*fard*, that which is obligatory according to the *shari'a*.

*fatwa* (pl. *fatawa*), a ruling or opinion in Islamic law given by a scholar or jurist.

*faylahsuf* (pl. *falasifah*), man or woman engaged in speculative philosophy or theology.

*fiqh*, Islamic law

*hadith*, a report of the sayings or deeds of the prophet, part of the *sunnah* of the prophet.

*hajj*, pilgrimage to the house of God

*halāl*, food which may be eaten because it was prepared according to Islamic law.

*harām*, forbidden

*hashr*, the gathering of all creatures to be judged

*hijāb*, Islamic dress, particularly that which covers a woman's hair and all of her body except hands, feet, and face.

*hijrah*, migration of Muhammad and his followers to Yathrib.

*ijithād*, exerting oneself to discover God's law free of received opinions.

*ijma*, consensus.

*Imam*, The supreme leader of the Muslim community. Used by Shiites to designate the true successors to Ali' and Hussein. Also used for the worship leader in a mosque.

*īmān*, faith, fidelity, belief

*Injil*, The teaching of Jesus.

*istighfār*, seeking pardon from mistakes or sins.

*istihsān*, judging something to be good

*jāhiliyya*, ignorance, the situation of the Arab peoples before the coming of Islam.

*al-Jannah*, The garden, paradise, the original home of humanity to which the righteous will return.

*jihād*, literally effort or exertion, usually associated with the struggle to establish Islam.

*jinn*, spirit beings said to be composed of vapors or flames and residing in their own realm, but able to influence human events, usually for ill.

*Ka'bah*, central sanctuary of Islam, located in Mecca.

*kāfir*, unbeliever in the sense of one unaware of or ungrateful for God and God's gifts.

*makrūh*, discouraged by the *shari'a*.

*mubāh*, indifferent by the *shari'a*.

*muezzin*, the one who makes the call to prayer from the minaret or door of the mosque.

*mustahabb*, encouraged by the *shari'a*

*näss*, in Shiite terminology the succession of the Imams, along with the appropriate knowledge and power.

*nūr*, light.

*pīr*, title for the leader of a Sufi *tarīqah*.

*purdah*, term used in Pakistan and Afghanistan for covering or veiling of women.

*qadā'/qadar*, the will of god and its implementation.

*qādi*, judge in *shari'a* law.

*qiyāmah*, Day of Judgment, Day of Resurrection.

*qiyās*, analogical reasoning.

*rasūl*, Messenger, the Prophet of God.

*ra'y*, personal opinion as a basis for ruling in Islamic law.

*riddah*, apostasy.

*salafiyya*, a movement to return to the "pious fathers" of Islam for models of legal and social development.

*shahādah*, witness, the Muslim profession of faith, "There is one God Allah and Muhammad is his Prophet."

*Shari'a*, divine law

*Shiite*, follower of the branch of Islam which regards Ali' and descendents as the true leaders of the Muslim community.

*shirk*, association, the sin of making anything or anyone equal to God.

*shura*, consultation as a principle by which Muslims should make decisions.

*Sirah*, (pl. *sīrat*), biography, especially of the Prophet.

*siyāsa shari'a*, governance in conformity with divine law, although not always directly from divine law.

*sufi*, Muslim mystic.

*sunnah*, tradition, in particular the tradition of the Prophet Muhammad's words and deeds.

*Sunni*, Those who base their Islam on the *sunnah* and accept the historical succession to the Caliphate through Mu'wiyyah and his successors.

*surah*, A chapter in the Quran.

*tafsīr*, interpretation.

*taqwā*, fear of God, piety.

*ta'wīl*, allegorical or esoteric interpretation of the Quran.

*tarīqah*, a way, a particular school of esoteric knowledge and practice in Sufism.

*tasliya*, blessing the Prophet.

*Taurat*, the law of Moses.

*tawba*, repentance, turning to God.

*tawhīd*, the unity of the divine being.

*tasawwuf*, esoteric teaching.

*'ulamā*, (singular *'alim*) collective term for the learned men of Islam.

*ummah*, people or community, the entire body of Muslims.

*usūl*, roots, especially the four roots of Divine law: Quran, Sunnah, qiyās, ijma.

*wahdat al-wujūd*, the unity of being.

*Zabūr*, the Psalms of David.

*zakāt*, the required tax, one of the five pillars of Islam.

# Maps

## The Early Expansion of Islam

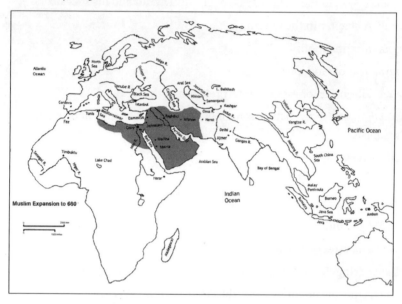

## The Muslim World in 1500

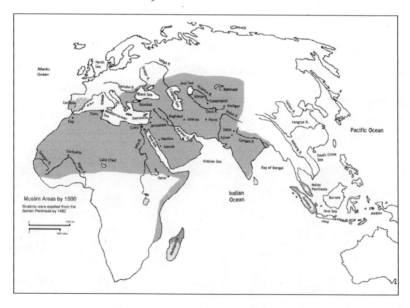

## Muslim Expansion to 1700

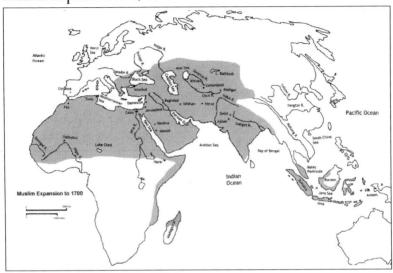

## Map of the Muslim World under Colonial Rule

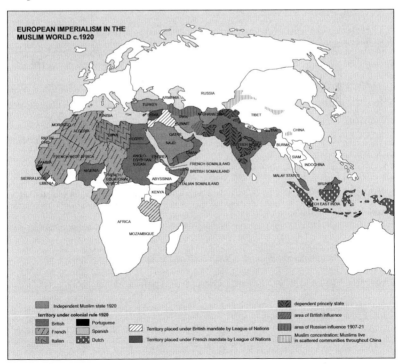

# Appendices

## Appendix A—The Pilgrimage

The pilgrimage begins on the eighth day of the month of the pilgrimage. Having arrived in Mecca, the pilgrim bathes and puts aside normal clothing and dons the pure white robe of a pilgrim. There is no distinction in dress among the millions who go on the pilgrimage. Having changed clothes, the pilgrim makes a first circuit of the *Ka'bah*, stopping for prayer. Next the pilgrim goes to drink water from the well of *Zamzam*. This is reputed to be the same water which saved Hagar and her infant son Ishmael in the desert (as found in Genesis 16:7). After spending the night in prayer the pilgrim goes on to Arafat, a hill outside Mecca, on the ninth day. Here the day in prayer focusing on the *talbiyah*:

"Here am I God! Here am I! Here am I, God! Here am I! And associate none with Thee; here am I! Surely Praise and Blessing are Thine, and dominion! And associate none with Thee, here am I God! Here am I!"

On the tenth day the pilgrim travels with other pilgrims to Mina. There they gather and throw small stones at three pillars that symbolize the temptations of Satan. On this or any subsequent day each pilgrim offers a sacrifice of camel, ox, or goat. This is followed by a visit to Mecca to once again circumambulate the *Ka'bah*. Then the pilgrims return to Mina once more for prayer and ritual stone-throwing. The pilgrimage can end on the twelfth day or later, and is usually concluded with a last ritual circumambulation of the *Ka'bah*.

## Appendix B—The Treaty of Umar

In the name of God, the Merciful, the Compassionate!

This is a writing to Umar from the Christians of such and such a city. When You [Muslims] marched against us [Christians]: we asked of you protection for ourselves, our posterity, our possessions, and our co-religionists;

and we made this stipulation with you, that we will not erect in our city or the suburbs any new monastery, church, cell or hermitage; that we will not repair any of such buildings that may fall into ruins, or renew those that may be situated in the Muslim quarters of the town; that we will not refuse the Muslims entry into our churches either by night or by day; that we will open the gates wide to passengers and travellers; that we will receive any Muslim traveller into our houses and give him food and lodging for three nights; that we will not harbor any spy in our churches or houses, or conceal any enemy of the Muslims.

That we will not teach our children the Qu'ran [some nationalist Arabs feared the infidels would ridicule the Qu'ran; others did not want infidels even to learn the language]; that we will not make a show of the Christian religion nor invite any one to embrace it; that we will not prevent any of our kinsmen from embracing Islam, if they so desire. That we will honor the Muslims and rise up in our assemblies when they wish to take their seats; that we will not imitate them in our dress, either in the cap, turban, sandals, or parting of the hair; that we will not make use of their expressions of speech, nor adopt their surnames [infidels must not use greetings and special phrases employed only by Muslims]; that we will not ride on saddles, or gird on swords, or take to ourselves arms or wear them, or engrave Arabic inscriptions on our rings; that we will not sell wine [forbidden to Muslims]; that we will shave the front of our heads; that we will keep to our own style of dress, wherever we may be; that we will wear girdles round our waists [infidels wore leather or cord girdles; Muslims, cloth and silk].

That we will not display the cross upon our churches or display our crosses or our sacred books in the streets of the Muslims, or in their market-places; that we will strike the clappers in our churches lightly [wooden rattles or bells summoned the people to church or synagogue]; that we will not recite our services in a loud voice when a Muslim is present; that we will not carry Palm branches [on Palm Sunday] or our images in procession in the streets; that at the burial of our dead we will not chant loudly or carry lighted candles in the streets of the Muslims or their market places; that we will not take any slaves that have already been in the possession of Muslims, nor spy into their houses; and that we will not strike any Muslim.

All this we promise to observe, on behalf of ourselves and our co-religionists, and receive protection from you in exchange; and if we violate any of the conditions of this agreement, then we forfeit your protection and you are at liberty to treat us as enemies and rebels.

(The source of this text is Jacob Marcus, *The Jew in the Medieval World: A Sourcebook, 315–1791,* (New York: JPS, 1938), 13–15. It is found in electronic form at http://www.fordham.edu/halsall/jewish/jews-umar. html. There are several other texts of this treaty in different medieval collections of Islamic law.)

## Appendix C—The Marrakesh Declaration of 2016

Executive Summary of the Marrakesh Declaration on the Rights of Religious Minorities in Predominantly Muslim Majority Communities—25th-27th January 2016

WHEREAS, conditions in various parts of the Muslim World have deteriorated dangerously due to the use of violence and armed struggle as a tool for settling conflicts and imposing one's point of view;

WHEREAS, this situation has also weakened the authority of legitimate governments and enabled criminal groups to issue edicts attributed to Islam, but which, in fact, alarmingly distort its fundamental principles and goals in ways that have seriously harmed the population as a whole;

WHEREAS, this year marks the 1,400th anniversary of the Charter of Medina, a constitutional contract between the Prophet Muhammad, God's peace and blessings be upon him, and the people of Medina, which guaranteed the religious liberty of all, regardless of faith;

WHEREAS, hundreds of Muslim scholars and intellectuals from over 120 countries, along with representatives of Islamic and international organizations, as well as leaders from diverse religious groups and nationalities, gathered in Marrakesh on this date to reaffirm the principles of the Charter of Medina at a major conference;

WHEREAS, this conference was held under the auspices of His Majesty, King Mohammed VI of Morocco, and organized jointly by the Ministry of Endowment and Islamic Affairs in the Kingdom of Morocco and the Forum for Promoting Peace in Muslim Societies based in the United Arab Emirates;

AND NOTING the gravity of this situation afflicting Muslims as well as peoples of other faiths throughout the world, and after thorough deliberation and discussion, the convened Muslim scholars and intellectuals:

DECLARE HEREBY our firm commitment to the principles articulated in the Charter of Medina, whose provisions contained a number of the principles of constitutional contractual citizenship, such as freedom of movement, property ownership, mutual solidarity and defense, as well as principles of justice and equality before the law; and that,

The objectives of the Charter of Medina provide a suitable framework for national constitutions in countries with Muslim majorities, and the United Nations Charter and related documents, such as

the Universal Declaration of Human Rights, are in harmony with the Charter of Medina, including consideration for public order.

NOTING FURTHER that deep reflection upon the various crises afflicting humanity underscores the inevitable and urgent need for cooperation among all religious groups, we

AFFIRM HEREBY that such cooperation must be based on a "Common Word," requiring that such cooperation must go beyond mutual tolerance and respect, to providing full protection for the rights and liberties to all religious groups in a civilized manner that eschews coercion, bias, and arrogance.

BASED ON ALL OF THE ABOVE, we hereby:

Call upon Muslim scholars and intellectuals around the world to develop a jurisprudence of the concept of "citizenship" which is inclusive of diverse groups. Such jurisprudence shall be rooted in Islamic tradition and principles and mindful of global changes.

Urge Muslim educational institutions and authorities to conduct a courageous review of educational curricula that addresses honestly and effectively any material that instigates aggression and extremism, leads to war and chaos, and results in the destruction of our shared societies;

Call upon politicians and decision makers to take the political and legal steps necessary to establish a constitutional contractual relationship among its citizens, and to support all formulations and initiatives that aim to fortify relations and understanding among the various religious groups in the Muslim World;

Call upon the educated, artistic, and creative members of our societies, as well as organizations of civil society, to establish a broad movement for the just treatment of religious minorities in Muslim countries and to raise awareness as to their rights, and to work together to ensure the success of these efforts.

Call upon the various religious groups bound by the same national fabric to address their mutual state of selective amnesia that blocks memories of centuries of joint and shared living on the same land; we call upon them to rebuild the past by reviving this tradition of conviviality, and restoring our shared trust that has been eroded by extremists using acts of terror and aggression;

Call upon representatives of the various religions, sects and denominations to confront all forms of religious bigotry, villification, and denegration of what people hold sacred, as well as all speech that promote hatred and bigotry; AND FINALLY,

AFFIRM that it is unconscionable to employ religion for the purpose of aggressing upon the rights of religious minorities in Muslim countries.

Marrakesh
January 2016 ,27th

## Appendix D—Muslim Festivals and the Muslim Ideal

Muslim religious ideals are expressed in the most commonly celebrated religious festivals. The following are commonly celebrated.

| Date | Name of Celebration | Type of Celebration |
| --- | --- | --- |
| 1, Muharram | Hijra, New Year | The beginning of the new year commemorates the Muslim migration from Mecca to Medina. In many Muslim lands this is an opportunity to stress the challenges of the coming year, so that "migration" becomes the ideal for progress and advancement |
| 10, Muharram | Ashura' | This Shi'a holiday commemorates the martyrdom of Imam Hussein. Shiites celebrate with mourning and sometimes extravagant self-inflicted pain. |

| Date | Name of Celebration | Type of Celebration |
| --- | --- | --- |
| 12, Rabi' I | Mawlid an Nabi | The birthday of the Prophet Muhammad (Peace be upon Him). |
| 27, Rajab | Lailat al Miraj | The Ascent of the Prophet to heaven on a winged horse. |
| 15, Sha'ban | Lailat al Bara'a | A night on which the destinies for the coming year are fixed, and past sins are absolved. It is the occasion of intense prayer. |
| Ramadan | | Month of fasting. Believers should consume no food, drink, or tobacco from sunrise to sunset. The fast begins each day at dawn, which is defined not by sunrise, but by the first light. Keeping this fast is commanded in the Quran, and Ramadan is a chance to live up to the ideal of submission to God which is basic to Islam. It is also a time for remembering the poor and offering hospitality. |
| 27, Ramadan | Lailat al Qadr | The Night of destiny, when Muhammad first received the revelation of the Quran. It is celebrated by all night recitations of the Quran. |
| 1, Shawwal | 'Id al Fitr | This feast marks the end of Ramadan. It commonly lasts three days and focuses on the ideals of family and community. |
| Dhu al Hijja | | This is the month of the pilgrimage to Mecca, another ritual commanded by God. For Muslims it is a chance to walk in the footsteps of Abraham and Muhammad, and to fulfill their submission to God's will by worshipping at the Ka'bah. |
| 8th, 9th, 10th of Dhu al Hijja | | The three official days of the pilgrimage. |

| Date | Name of Celebration | Type of Celebration |
|------|--------------------|--------------------|
| 10, Dhu al Hijja | 'Id al Adha | Festival of sacrifice. The culmination of the Hajj or holy pilgrimage. Those who have made the pilgrimage will continue to sacrifice a goat or lamb and share it with their neighbors when they return home, remembering the ideal of community solidarity. |

## Appendix E—The Ninety-Nine Names of God

al-Awwal, The First

al-Ākhir, The Last

al-Ahad, The One

al-Badī, The Originator

al-Bari, The Producer

al-Barr, The Beneficent

al-Basīr, The Seeing

al-Bāsit, The Expander

al-Bātin, The Inner

al-Ba'ith, The Raiser

al-Bāqī, The Enduring

al-Tawwāb, The Relenting

al-Jabbār, The Irresistible

al-Jalīl, The Majestic

al-Jāmi, The Gatherer

al-Hasīb, The Accounter

al-Hāfiz, The Guardian

al-Haqq, The Truth

al-Hakīm, The Wise

al-Hakam, The Judge

al-Halīm, The Kindly

al-Hamīd, The Praiseworthy

al-Hayy, The Living

al-Khabīr, The Well-Informed

al-Khāfid, The Abaser

al-Khāliq, The Creator

Dhu-l-Jalāl wa-l-Ikrām, Full of Majesty and Generosity

ar-Ra'ūf, The Gentle

ar-Rahmān, The Merciful

ar-Rahīm, The Compassionate

ar-Razzāq, The Provider

ar-Rashīd, The Guide

ar-Rāfi, The Exalter

ar-Raqīb, The Vigilant

as-Salām, The Peace

as-Samī, The Hearer

ash-Shakūr, The Grateful

ash-Shahīd, The Witness

ash-Sabūr, The Forbearing

ash-Samad, The Eternal

ad-Darr, The Afflicter

az-Zāhir, The Outer

al-'Adl, The Just

al-'Azīz, The Mighty, The Precious

al-'Azīm, The Great

al-'Afuw, The Pardoner

al-'Alīm, The Knowing

al-'Alī, The High One

al-Ghafūr, The Forgiver

al-Ghaffār, The Forgiving

al-Ghānī, The Rich

al-Fattāh, The Opener

al-Qabid, The Seizer

al-Qadīr, The Capable

al-Quddūs, The Holy

al-Qahhār, The Victorious

al-Qawī, The Strong

al-Qayyūm, The Self-Subsistent

al-Kabīr, The Great

al-Karīm, The Generous, The Noble

al-Latīf, The Gracious

al-Muta'akhkhir, The Deferrer

al-Mu'min, The Believer

al-Muta'alī, The Self-Exalted

al-Mutakkabir, The Superb

al-Matīn, The Firm

al-Mubdi', The Founder

al-Mujīb, The Responsive

al-Majīd, The Glorious

al-Muhsi, The Counterer

al-Muhyī, The Giver of Life

al-Mudhill, The Abaser

al-Muzīl, The Separator

al-Musawwir, The Shaper

al-Mu'īd, The Restorer

al-Mu'izz, The Honorer

al-Mu'tī, The Giver

al-Mughnī, The Enricher

al-Muqīt, The Maintainer

al-Muqtadir, The Prevailer

al-Muqaddim, The Bringer Forward

al-Muqsit, The Equitable

al-Malik, The King

Malik al-Mulk, Possessor of the Kingdom

al-Mumīt, The Slayer

al-Muntaqim, The Avenger

al-Muhaimin, The Vigilant

an-Nāfi, The Propitious

an-Nāsir, The Helper

an-Nūr, The Light

al-Hādi, The Guide

al-Wāhid, The Unique

al-Wadūd, The Loving

al-Wārith, The Inheritor

al-Wāsi, The Vast

al-Wakīl, The Steward

al-Walīy, The Patron

al-Wāli, The Protector

al-Wahhāb, The Bestower

# Bibliography and Suggested Reading

## Islamic Ideals

The recommended reading list below focuses on books in which Muslims focus on the ideals being discussed in this book. In the end the only way to understand and appreciate Muslims and their religion is by listening to their voice.

Corbin, Henry. Alone with the Alone: Creative Imagination in the Sūfism of Ibn 'Arabī / Henry Corbin. With a New Preface by Harold Bloom. Princeton, NJ: Princeton University Press, 1999.

Cragg, Kenneth. *The Event of the Quran*. Oxford: Oneworld, 1994. A classic and sympathetic introduction to an Islamic ideal by a Christian author.

Drosnin, Michael. *The Bible Code*. New York: Orion, 1997.

Mawdudi, Abul A'la. *Towards Understanding Islam*. Leicester: The Islamic Foundation, 1980.

Mernissi, Fatima. *Beyond the Veil*. London: Virago, 1993.

———. *Islam and Democracy*. New York: Basic, 2002.

Muslim Bin al-Hajjaj, A. A. H., and A. H. Siddiqi. Sahih Muslim. Lahore, Pakistan: Ashraf, 1976.

Nasr, Seyyed Hossein, ed. *Islamic Spirituality*, vols. I and II. New York: Crossroad, 1987.

Padwick, Constance E. *Muslim Devotions*. Oxford: Oneworld, 1997. Although not by a Muslim, there are few books in English that so eloquently or sympathetically introduce the ritual and meaning of Muslim prayer to Christian readers. This is a classic.

Qutb, Sayyid. *Milestones*. Indianapolis: American Trust, 1990.

Rahman, Fazlur. *Islam and Modernity*. Chicago: University of Chicago Press, 1982.

Ramadan, Tariq. *To Be a European Muslim: A Study of Islamic Sources in the European Context*. Leicester: The Islamic Foundation, 1999.

———. *Radical Reform: Islamic Ethics and Liberation*. Oxford: Oxford University Press, 2009.

Robinson, Neal. Discovering the Qur'an: a Contemporary Approach to a Veiled Text. London: SCM, 1996.

Sardar, Ziauddin. Islamic Futures: The Shape of Ideas to Come. Selangor Darul Ehsan, Malaysia: Pelanduk, 1988.

Taylor, Charles. *Modern Social Imaginaries*. Public Planet Books. Durham, NC: Duke University Press, 2003.

Wadud-Muhsin, Amina. *Quran and Woman*. Shah Alam, Malaysia: Penerbit Fajar Bakti, 1992.